Simply Perfect
Every Time

David Herbert has been obsessed with food since childhood. Growing up in a small seaside town, his spare time was spent fishing and thinking of new ways to cook his daily catch.

David is the author of the bestselling book *Picnics*, and contributes recipes to numerous magazines and newspapers. He is currently working and living in London, surrounded by his kitchen treasures, cookbooks and copper saucepans.

Simply Perfect Every Time

130 Classic, Foolproof Recipes

David Herbert

photographs by Andre Martin

MARLOWE & COMPANY
New York

SIMPLY PERFECT EVERY TIME: *130 Classic, Foolproof Recipes*

Copyright © 2003, 2004 by David Herbert
Photographs copyright © 2003 by Andre Martin

AVALON
publishing group incorporated

Published by
Marlowe & Company
An Imprint of Avalon Publishing Group Incorporated
245 West 17th Street, 11th Floor
New York, NY 10011-5300

Originally published as *The Perfect Cookbook* by Penguin Books Australia Ltd in 2003.
This is a revised edition, adapted for North America and published by arrangement.

Library of Congress Cataloging-in-Publication Data
Herbert, David (David John)
[Perfect cookbook]
Simply perfect every time: 130 classic, foolproof recipes / by David Herbert.
p. cm.
Originally published: The perfect cookbook. Australia: Penguin Books Australia, 2003.
Includes index.
ISBN 1-56924-410-3
1. Cookery. I. Title
TX714.H4656 2004
641.5—dc22   2004057900

9 8 7 6 5 4 3 2 1

Designed by Pauline Neuwirth, Neuwirth & Associates, Inc.,
modified from a design by Louise Leffler, Penguin Design Studios

Printed in Canada
Distributed by Publishers Group West

*For Sally, JoAnn, Pat, and Frankie
in anticipation of many happy
Thanksgiving feasts.*

introduction

I cannot remember a time when I didn't collect recipes or hoard cookbooks. My favorite recipes, altered and adjusted over time, have ended up in a series of handwritten notebooks. Little books of souvenirs—full of memories, dog-eared corners, crossings out, and smudges of cake batter.

When I was first asked to write a weekly recipe column for a local newspaper, I turned directly to these notebooks. The only catch: the newspaper had limited space, so I was only allowed 150 words for each recipe. Undaunted, I worked hard to choose classic recipes that were interesting, approachable, and that would work *every* time. I still remember the first recipe that I wrote, for roast chicken. I tested the recipe over and over to make sure it was just right—it took me nearly a week to reduce it to 144 words. It remains one of my most requested favorites.

Simply Perfect Every Time has grown out of that collection of well-loved dishes written for the newspaper. The 130 recipes here reflect my approach to cooking and eating—simple, nostalgic, eclectic, but never fussy or difficult.

Just as I did with the roast chicken recipe, I've tested each recipe in this book repeatedly to make absolutely certain that it comes out perfectly every time. Anything that was too complicated, demanding, or lengthy did not make the cut. The bottom line was that the recipes had to be foolproof and the dishes had to stand the test of time.

So cook them, enjoy them, change them to suit your individual tastes and use them as a base to expand your skills. Experiment! After all, it's only food. I encourage you to approach these recipes with a sense of fun, not with anxiety—and to use good quality seasonal ingredients. I promise, you can't go wrong!

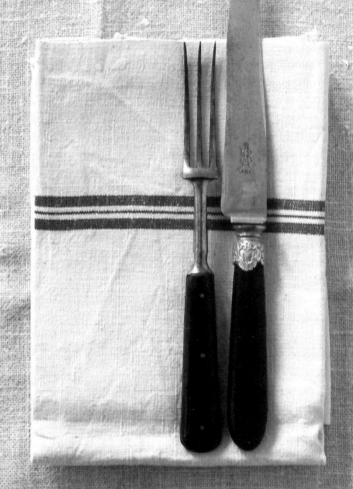

an a-z of simply perfect recipes

almond cakes.

These delicious, moist almond cakes are easy to make at home.

¾ cup unsalted butter	2 teaspoons finely grated lemon zest
⅓ cup plain (all-purpose) flour	5 egg whites
6 ounces confectioners' sugar	confectioners' sugar, extra, to serve
¾ cup ground almonds	

- Preheat the oven to 400°F. Lightly grease a 6-cup muffin pan.

- Melt the butter in a small saucepan over low heat, then cook for 1 minute longer, or until golden. Be careful not to burn the butter.

- Sift the flour and confectioners' sugar into a mixing bowl. Stir in the ground almonds and lemon zest.

- Lightly beat the egg whites with a fork and pour into the bowl containing the dry ingredients. Add the warm butter and mix with a wooden spoon until smooth.

- Spoon the mixture into the prepared muffin pan, filling each to three-quarters full. Bake for 5 minutes, then reduce the heat to 350°F and bake for 10–15 minutes longer, or until golden and risen.

- Allow to cool in the pan for 5 minutes before turning out onto a wire rack to cool completely. Dust with confectioners' sugar to serve.

In place of the lemon zest, try orange zest.

—

To make berry cakes, top each with a few fresh or frozen raspberries, blackberries, or blueberries before baking.

MAKES 8

angel food cake.

12 egg whites	1 teaspoon vanilla extract
1 teaspoon cream of tartar	1 cup plain (all-purpose) flour, divided
pinch of salt	1 teaspoon baking powder
1½ cups sugar, divided	confectioners' sugar, to dust

- Have an ungreased angel food cake pan (tube pan) ready.

- Move the oven rack to the lowest position and preheat the oven to 350°F.

- Place the egg whites, cream of tartar, and salt into a large bowl. With an electric mixer, on medium speed, beat the egg whites and cream of tartar until the egg whites form stiff peaks (if you lift the mixer out of the bowl, the mixture will cling to the beaters, keeping stiff and moist looking peaks).

- Continue to beat the mixture, gradually adding half of the sugar, one tablespoon at a time. Continue beating the mixture and adding the sugar until all of the sugar is added and the mixture is stiff and glossy (this may take from 5 to 10 minutes). Fold in the vanilla extract.

- Sift in half the flour, baking powder, and half of the remaining sugar. Fold in gently with a large spoon. Repeat with the remaining flour and sugar.

- Spoon into the pan and bake for 35–40 minutes, or until lightly golden and the top of the cake springs back when touched. A wooden skewer inserted into the cake should come out clean.

- Turn the cake pan upside-down, or if you prefer, rest the cake on the neck of a heatproof funnel or bottle. Let hang for 2 hours or until the cake has completely cooled. Loosen the sides of the pan with a knife or long metal spatula, and then remove the cake. Serve dusted with confectioners' sugar.

SERVES 8

apple pie.

1 homemade regular shortcrust pastry (see page 119), or 1 12-ounce package (2 pie crusts)

frozen pie crust, thawed

5 large Granny Smith apples

2 tablespoons butter

½ cup sugar

1 tablespoon lemon juice

2 tablespoons cornstarch

1 teaspoon ground cinnamon

pinch of ground cloves

1 egg, beaten

sugar, extra, to sprinkle

- Prepare the pastry according to the instructions on page 119 and refrigerate for at least 30 minutes.

- Peel, core, and cut the apples into chunks.

- Melt the butter in a large saucepan and add the apples, sugar, lemon juice, and 1 tablespoon of water. Cook over medium heat for 5–7 minutes, or until the apples have softened. Taste and add extra sugar if needed.

- Sprinkle over the cornstarch and spices and cook, stirring well, for 1 minute longer. Set aside to cool.

- Preheat the oven to 375°F. Grease a 9" pie plate.

- Roll out two-thirds of the dough between two sheets of baking paper until large enough to line the base and sides of the plate. Line the plate with the pastry, allowing any excess to hang over the sides. Pile the apple mixture into the pastry shell.

- Roll out the remaining pastry until large enough to cover the pie. Place over the pie and press the edges together to seal. Make two incisions in the center of the lid for the steam to escape. Trim any overhanging pastry and brush the top of the pie with the beaten egg. Sprinkle the top with the extra sugar.

- Bake for 40 minutes, or until golden.

SERVES 8

apples, baked.

Cold winter nights are the times to revive this simple, old-fashioned treat.

6 Granny Smith or Jonathan apples	¾ cup coarsely chopped raisins
¼ cup lightly packed brown sugar	1 teaspoon finely grated orange zest
4 tablespoons unsalted butter, softened	½ teaspoon ground cinnamon
2 tablespoons chopped hazelnuts	2 tablespoons honey or golden syrup

- Preheat the oven to 350°F.

- Core the apples, leaving a slightly wider opening at the top than the bottom.

- Combine the brown sugar, butter, hazelnuts, raisins, orange zest, and cinnamon in a mixing bowl. Stuff the apples firmly with the mixture and pile any leftover filling on the top. Place the stuffed apples in a baking dish that holds them snugly.

- Spoon about 1 teaspoon of honey over each apple. Gently pour ⅓ cup of water into the bottom of the dish and bake for 30–40 minutes, or until the apples are soft.

- Serve drizzled with any syrup from the bottom of the dish. Accompany with a cup of thick cream.

Vary the filling by using different dried fruits or nuts. Raisins and almonds, or dried figs and walnuts, are good combinations.

—

Golden syrup is a liquid sweetener that imparts a rich, toasty flavor in cooking and baking. It is made from evaporated sugar cane juice and has the consistency of corn syrup. Look for golden syrup in gourmet food markets or substitute with honey, corn syrup, or light molasses. Alternately, try 2 parts light corn syrup and 1 part molasses.

SERVES 6

baked beans.

2 tablespoons vegetable oil	1 tablespoon brown sugar
6 slices smoked bacon, roughly chopped	$\frac{1}{2}$ teaspoon chili powder
1 small onion, finely chopped	1 13-ounce can navy or white beans, rinsed and drained
1 clove garlic, crushed	1 13-ounce can chopped or crushed tomatoes
2 tablespoons maple syrup	
2 teaspoons Dijon mustard	1 bay leaf

- Heat the oil in a large frying pan and cook the bacon for 2 minutes. Add the onion and garlic, stirring occasionally for 5 minutes or until the onion is soft and slightly translucent.

- Add the maple syrup, mustard, brown sugar, chili powder, beans, tomatoes, bay leaf, and $\frac{1}{2}$ cup of water.

- Simmer over low heat for 45 minutes, stirring occasionally. When finished, the mixture should be thick, but add extra water if needed during cooking. Remove the bay leaf and serve.

SERVES 4

baked custard.

2 cups milk	1 teaspoon vanilla extract
1 cup cream	½ cup sugar
3 eggs	¼ teaspoon ground nutmeg
2 egg yolks	

- Preheat the oven to 300°F.

- Combine the milk and cream in a medium-sized saucepan and heat gently until the mixture comes to a boil. Remove from the heat.

- Lightly beat the whole eggs, egg yolks, vanilla, and sugar in a bowl. Pour the hot cream mixture into the egg mixture, and whisk well. Transfer to a 6-cup-capacity ovenproof dish and sprinkle with the nutmeg.

- Stand the dish in a large baking pan and fill the pan with enough boiling water to come halfway up the sides of the dish. Carefully transfer to the oven and bake for 35–45 minutes, or until the custard has just set—it should still wobble a little. To test, insert a knife about 2" from the side of the dish; if it comes out clean, the custard is ready.

- Serve with fresh or poached fruit.

To make ginger-infused custard, add 1 teaspoon of grated fresh ginger to the cream mixture. Heat and allow the ginger to infuse for 10 minutes. Strain and make the custard as above.

—

Make individual custards by pouring the mixture into six small ramekins. Bake as above, but for 20–25 minutes only.

SERVES 4-6

banana bread.

1½ cups plain (all-purpose) flour	1 cup sugar
1 teaspoon baking powder	2 eggs, lightly beaten
1 teaspoon baking soda	2 large very ripe bananas
¼ teaspoon salt	½ cup buttermilk
½ cup unsalted butter, softened	confectioners' sugar, to serve

- Preheat the oven to 325°F. Grease a 9" x 5" loaf pan and line the base and sides with baking paper.

- Sift together the flour, baking powder, baking soda, and salt.

- In a separate bowl, use an electric mixer to beat the butter and sugar for 3–4 minutes, or until pale and fluffy. Gradually add the beaten eggs, mixing well after each addition.

- Mash the bananas with a fork and add to the butter mixture. Stir well to combine. Add the combined dry ingredients alternately with the buttermilk, beating well after each addition.

- Spoon the mixture into the prepared loaf pan and bake for 55–60 minutes, or until the top of the bread is firm and is a deep brown color. A wooden skewer inserted into the center should come out clean. Allow to cool in the pan for 10 minutes before turning out onto a wire rack.

- Serve dusted with confectioners' sugar. The flavor improves on keeping. Store for up to 3 days covered in plastic wrap.

Day-old banana bread is delicious cut into slices and toasted.
Substitute a mixture of ¼ cup plain yogurt and ¼ cup milk if you can't find buttermilk.

SERVES 12

banana pancakes.

1 cup plain (all-purpose) flour	2 eggs, lightly beaten
1 teaspoon baking powder	1 cup milk
2 tablespoons sugar	2 tablespoons butter, melted
pinch of salt	2 ripe bananas, peeled and thinly sliced

- Sift the flour, baking powder, sugar, and salt into a medium mixing bowl.

- In a separate bowl, combine the beaten eggs, milk, and melted butter. Pour the wet ingredients into the dry ingredients and mix until a smooth batter forms.

- Grease a non-stick frying pan or griddle with butter. Preheat the pan over medium heat for 1 minute.

- Ladle 3–4 tablespoons of batter for each pancake into the pan.

- Top each pancake with sliced bananas and cook for about 1 minute, or until bubbles appear on the pancake and the underside is golden. Using a spatula, flip the pancake over and cook for 45–60 seconds longer or until the pancake is puffed and becomes slightly dry around the edges. Repeat with the remaining batter. Serve with maple syrup and vanilla yogurt.

This pancake batter can be made ahead of time and left to rest for up to two hours.

SERVES 2-3

barley, bacon, and leek soup.

This is the sort of old-fashioned soup I love to make and eat during the cooler weather. It is nourishing, easily prepared and a meal in itself.

1 tablespoon vegetable oil	1 teaspoon fresh thyme
5 slices bacon, roughly chopped	1 bay leaf
2 large leeks, sliced into 1″ rounds	4 cups chicken stock
1 clove of garlic, chopped	½ cup pearl barley
2 carrots, sliced	2 tablespoons chopped parsley
2 ribs celery, sliced	

- Heat the oil in a large saucepan over medium heat. Add the bacon and cook, stirring for 3–4 minutes. Add the leeks, garlic, carrots, celery, thyme, and bay leaf. Cook for 7–10 minutes, stirring occasionally, or until the leeks have softened. Add the chicken stock, 2 cups of water, and the pearl barley. Bring to a boil then reduce the heat and simmer gently for about 60 minutes, skimming the surface with a spoon to remove any foam. Continue to cook for a few minutes longer or until the barley is soft and tender.

- Season to taste with salt and freshly ground pepper. Garnish with chopped parsley.

There is no need to be too skilled with a knife to make this soup—I slice the vegetables into approximately ¼″ pieces.

—

As a variation (and to add some fresh greens to the soup), add a large handful of chopped spinach or some frozen peas about 5 minutes before serving.

—

You can also add 1½ cups of cooked, chopped chicken about 10 minutes before serving. Be sure the chicken is thoroughly heated before ladling into soup bowls.

SERVES 4

beef casserole.

¼ cup plain (all-purpose) flour

3½ pounds rump or chuck steak, cut into ¾" cubes

⅓ cup olive oil

3 slices bacon, roughly chopped

8 small onions, peeled and quartered

2 cloves garlic, crushed

3 carrots, sliced

2 cups beef stock

2 cups red wine

1 13-ounce can chopped tomatoes

1 teaspoon finely grated orange zest

4 sprigs thyme

1 bay leaf

2 tablespoons chopped flat-leaf parsley

salt and freshly ground black pepper

- Preheat the oven to 325°F.

- Place the flour in a clean plastic bag. Shake a few pieces of meat in the bag until lightly dusted. Repeat with the remaining pieces of meat.

- Heat 2 tablespoons of the oil in a large frying pan over medium heat. Cook the steak in batches, adding a little extra oil if needed, until browned. Transfer to a large casserole dish.

- Heat the remaining 2 tablespoons of oil in the frying pan over medium heat. Add the bacon and cook for 2 minutes. Add the onions, garlic, and carrots, and cook, stirring occasionally, for 5 minutes, or until the onions are tender. Transfer to the casserole dish.

- Drain any fat from the frying pan, add the stock and bring to a boil for 1 minute. Stir to incorporate any bits stuck to the bottom of the pan. Transfer to the casserole dish and stir in the wine, tomatoes, orange zest, thyme, bay leaf, and parsley. Cover, transfer to the oven and cook for 3 hours. Stir the meat occasionally as it cooks.

- Remove from the oven and check the sauce. Add a little extra water if it appears dry. Alternatively, if the sauce is a little watery, uncover and return to the oven to allow the sauce to reduce. Season well with salt and freshly ground black pepper. Serve with mashed potatoes or buttered noodles and plenty of crusty bread.

SERVES 6

beef pot roast.

3½ - 4½ pounds of beef arm, blade or cross rib pot roast

2 tablespoons olive oil

2 medium onions, quartered

2 cloves garlic, peeled, whole

2 leeks, washed and white parts sliced into ½" rounds

2 carrots cut into 1" chunks

3 ribs celery, roughly chopped

2 bay leaves

1 teaspoon orange zest

½ cup red wine

2 cups beef or veal stock

4 sprigs thyme

- Preheat the oven to 325°F.

- Heat 1 tablespoon of oil in a large, heatproof casserole dish or Dutch oven over medium-high heat. Add the meat and brown on all sides. Transfer the meat to a plate while you cook the vegetables.

- Heat the remaining oil over medium heat.

- Add the onions, garlic, leeks, carrots and celery, and cook, stirring occasionally, for 5–6 minutes, or until the vegetables are tender. Add the beef, bay leaves, orange zest, and thyme.

- Pour in the wine and just enough stock to fill the casserole dish, leaving 2" of space at the top. Bring to a boil over medium heat. Cover, then transfer to the oven and cook for about 2½ hours. Baste the meat occasionally as it cooks.

- Remove the beef and vegetables from the dish and transfer to a serving platter. Set aside in a warm place. Skim off any fat from the surface of the sauce, adding a little extra water if dry. Alternatively, if the sauce is a little thin, uncover, bring to a slow boil and cook until reduced.

- Stir in the parsley and season to taste. Serve the beef sliced, accompanied with vegetables.

SERVES 8

biscotti.

¾ cup blanched almonds	1 teaspoon finely chopped rosemary
1½ cups plain (all-purpose) flour	2 eggs, beaten
1 teaspoon baking powder	1 egg yolk
1 cup sugar	1 teaspoon vanilla extract
2 teaspoons finely grated orange zest	

- Preheat the oven to 350°F.

- Spread the almonds in a single layer on an oven tray and bake for 7–10 minutes, tossing occasionally, until fragrant and lightly toasted. Cool and roughly chop.

- Sift the flour and baking powder into a mixing bowl. Stir in the sugar, orange zest, rosemary, and chopped almonds. Add the beaten eggs, egg yolk, and vanilla and mix to form a firm dough. If the dough is very sticky, add extra flour.

- Knead the dough on a lightly floured surface for 5 minutes, or until smooth. Form into a slightly flattened log about 12" in length. Place on an oven tray lined with baking paper and bake for 40 minutes, or until firm and golden. Allow to cool on a wire rack.

- Reduce the oven temperature to 275°F. Line two oven trays with baking paper.

- With a long serrated knife, carefully cut the log diagonally into ¼–½" thick slices. The slices will be crumbly on the edges, so work slowly.

- Arrange the biscotti in a single layer on the prepared oven trays and return them to the oven for 20–25 minutes, turning occasionally, until dry and crisp. Store in an airtight container for 2–3 weeks.

Try substituting pistachios or hazelnuts for the almonds, dry-roasting them as above.

MAKES 25-30

blueberry muffins.

2 cups plain (all-purpose) flour	2 large eggs
2 teaspoons baking powder	grated zest of 1 lemon
1 teaspoon baking soda	$^3/_4$ cup sugar
$^1/_8$ teaspoon salt	$^1/_2$ cup unsalted butter, melted
1$^1/_4$ cups buttermilk	1 cup fresh or frozen blueberries

- Preheat the oven to 375°F. Grease a 12-cup muffin pan or line with paper baking cups.

- Sift the flour, baking powder, baking soda, and salt into a mixing bowl.

- Whisk together the buttermilk, eggs, lemon zest, sugar, and melted butter. Pour the egg mixture into the flour mixture and stir until the ingredients are just combined. Do not over-mix; the batter should not be smooth (lumps are fine here). Lightly fold in the fruit.

- Divide the mixture evenly between the muffin cups.

- Bake for 20–25 minutes, or until the top of the muffin is golden in color and a wooden skewer inserted into the center comes out clean. Allow to cool in the pan for 5 minutes before placing on a wire rack. Serve warm.

If you can't find buttermilk, use ½ cup of plain yogurt mixed with ½ cup of milk.

—

To make nut muffins, fold in ½–¾ cup of chopped pecans. Sprinkle the top of each muffin with a little ground cinnamon and add some extra chopped nuts before baking.

—

To make pear and lemon muffins, fold in 1¼ cups of diced pears in place of the blueberries. Sprinkle the top of each muffin with brown sugar before baking.

MAKES 12

bolognese sauce.

Serve this versatile sauce with spaghetti, polenta, baked potatoes,
or simply enjoy it hot on toast.

2 tablespoons olive oil	2 13-ounce cans crushed tomatoes
1 onion, finely chopped	1 cup beef stock
1 carrot, chopped	2 tablespoons tomato paste
1 clove garlic, crushed	$\frac{1}{2}$ teaspoon dried oregano
1 pound ground beef	pinch of ground nutmeg
$\frac{1}{2}$ cup red wine	salt and freshly ground black pepper

- Heat the olive oil in a large saucepan and gently sauté the onion and carrot for 5 minutes, or until tender and slightly golden.

- Add the garlic and ground beef to the vegetable mixture. Cook until the meat starts to brown. Break up any lumps of meat with a fork.

- Add the red wine and cook, stirring frequently, until almost evaporated. Add the remaining ingredients except the salt and pepper. Cook, stirring occasionally, over low heat for $1\frac{1}{2}$ hours.

- Season with salt and freshly ground black pepper, and serve.

*For a more robust flavor, add 4 ounces of finely chopped pancetta to the
vegetable mixture at the beginning.*

—

*Bolognese sauce can be made in large quantities and frozen in small portions
for up to 3 months.*

SERVES 4-6

bread.

1¼-ounce package (2¼ teaspoons) active dry yeast

1 teaspoon sugar

4 cups bread flour

salt

1 tablespoon olive oil

- Dissolve the yeast and sugar in a small cup with ½ cup of warm water. Stir well and leave for 10 minutes, or until the mixture froths.

- Place the flour and a pinch of salt in a large mixing bowl. Make a well in the center and add the yeast mixture, olive oil, and 1 cup of warm water. Mix until a firm dough forms. Add a little extra water if the dough is too dry.

- Knead the dough on a lightly floured surface for 10–15 minutes, or until smooth and elastic. Place in a clean, lightly oiled bowl, cover with a cloth or plastic wrap and leave in a warm place for 1–1½ hours, or until the dough has doubled in size.

- Punch down the dough with your fist to expel the air. Knead on a lightly floured surface for 2 minutes, or until smooth. Place the dough in a greased 9" x 5" x 3" loaf pan.

- Cover and leave for 45–60 minutes, or until the dough has doubled in size.

- Preheat the oven to 400°F.

- Slash the top of the loaf a couple of times with a sharp knife. Bake for 40 minutes, or until the loaf has risen and is golden brown. Turn out the loaf, place on an oven tray and return it to the oven for 5 minutes. When baked, the loaf should be golden and sound hollow when tapped on the bottom. Allow to cool on a wire rack.

Only use bread-making flour or a high-gluten blend, available from health-food stores or from the health-food section of supermarkets. Alternatively, look for bread flour at farmers' markets or a local mill. Plain flour does not contain enough gluten, which gives the dough its elasticity.

—

Instead of making a loaf, shape the dough into whatever shapes you like and bake directly on an oven tray.

—

Experiment by replacing some of the white flour with whole-grain or rye flour.

ONE LOAF; 16 SLICES

bread sticks.

1¼-ounce package (2¼ teaspoons) active dry yeast

1 teaspoon sugar

¾ cup warm water (120°F to 130°F)

2 cups bread flour

½ teaspoon salt

2 tablespoons parmesan, finely grated

2 tablespoons olive oil

1 teaspoon fresh thyme, finely chopped

extra olive oil, to brush

sea salt, to sprinkle

- Dissolve the yeast and sugar in a small cup of warm water. Stir well and let stand for 10 minutes until bubbly.

- Place the flour, salt, and half of the parmesan into the bowl of an electric mixer. Add the yeast and olive oil. Mix with a dough hook on medium speed until a firm dough forms. Add a little extra water if the dough is too dry. Mix for a few minutes longer until smooth and elastic.

- Knead on a lightly floured surface for 2 minutes, then place the dough in a lightly oiled bowl. Cover the bowl with plastic wrap and leave in a warm place for 1 hour, or until the dough has doubled in size.

- Punch down the dough with your fist to expel the air; then knead on a lightly floured surface for 2 minutes.

- Pinch off large walnut-sized pieces of dough and roll each by hand into long thin sticks. Place on a large, greased baking sheet. Brush each stick with a little extra oil and sprinkle with salt and the remaining parmesan. Set aside in a warm place for 15 minutes.

- Meanwhile, preheat the oven to 400°F.

- Bake for 10–15 minutes, or until crisp and golden brown.

The best bread sticks are made using bread-making flour or a high-gluten blend. Look for quality bread flour in health food shops or in the health-food section of supermarkets.

MAKES 20

caesar salad.

5 slices bacon, chopped

4 thick slices white bread

1 tablespoon vegetable oil

2 small heads Romaine lettuce

½ cup freshly shaved parmesan

DRESSING

4 anchovy fillets

1 clove garlic, crushed

2 tablespoons lemon juice

1 egg yolk

½ teaspoon Dijon mustard

¼ cup olive oil

salt and freshly ground black pepper

- Cook the bacon in a large frying pan over medium heat for 5 minutes, or until crisp. Drain on kitchen paper.

- Remove the crusts from the bread and cut the bread into ¾" cubes. Add the oil to the frying pan and fry the bread over medium heat, tossing constantly, until golden brown. Drain the croutons on kitchen paper.

- To make the dressing, place all of the ingredients except the salt and pepper in a blender and pulse until combined. Season to taste with salt and freshly ground black pepper.

- Separate the lettuce leaves, rinse well, and dry with a clean tea towel. Place the leaves in a serving bowl, sprinkle over the bacon and croutons, and drizzle over the dressing. Finish with a sprinkle of shaved parmesan.

You can make chicken caesar salad by adding two cooked and roughly chopped boneless, skinless chicken breasts to this salad.

SERVES 4

caramel oranges.

I love the simplicity of this dish—especially during the winter months when oranges are at their peak and their sweetest.

6 oranges	⅓ cup sugar
2 tablespoons liqueur, such as Grand Marnier, Cointreau, or vodka	

- Using a sharp knife, peel away the skin and any bitter pith from the oranges. Do this over a small bowl—this way you can collect any juice.

- Slice the oranges into thin, 1¼" slices, again, saving any juice. Add the orange slices and the liqueur to the bowl of juice.

- Chill for about 30 minutes, turning occasionally.

- Meanwhile, make a caramel by combining the sugar and 1/4 cup of water in a small saucepan. Place over medium heat and bring to a boil, stirring to dissolve the sugar. Reduce the heat and simmer, without stirring, for 5–10 minutes, or until the liquid is a deep, golden caramel color. Watch the caramel constantly as it can burn easily and avoid the temptation to stir it.

- Remove from the heat when ready. Allow to stand for a couple of minutes to thicken slightly. If the caramel continues to bubble after removing from the heat, place the base of the saucepan into a sink of cold water to stop the cooking process.

- When ready to serve, arrange the chilled orange slices between 4 plates and pour the juice over the fruit. Additionally, pour enough of the caramel over the oranges to lightly coat them. Let the fruit sit for a minute, and then serve.

This recipe works well using blood oranges—a sweet-tart, red-fleshed orange, available in farmers' markets or in the produce section of most supermarkets.

SERVES 4

carrot cake.

2 cups plain (all-purpose) flour

1½ teaspoons baking powder

1 teaspoon baking soda

½ teaspoon ground cinnamon

⅛ teaspoon salt

4 eggs, lightly beaten

1½ cups lightly packed brown sugar

¾ cup vegetable oil

⅓ cup honey or golden syrup

2½ cups firmly packed grated carrot

½ cup drained crushed canned pineapple

½ cup chopped pecans or walnuts

- Preheat the oven to 325°F. Lightly grease a 9" round cake pan and line the base with baking paper.

- In a small mixing bowl, combine the flour, baking powder, baking soda, cinnamon, and salt.

- In a large mixing bowl, lightly whisk together the eggs and brown sugar until the sugar has dissolved and the mixture is frothy. Stir in the oil and honey and mix with a wooden spoon until smooth.

- Sift the flour mixture into the egg mixture and mix until smooth. Stir in the carrot, pineapple, and pecans or walnuts.

- Spoon the mixture into the prepared cake pan and level the top. Bake for 1–1¼ hours, or until golden and firm to the touch. A wooden skewer inserted into the center should come out clean.

- Allow to cool in the pan for 10 minutes before turning out onto a wire rack to cool completely. Serve dusted with confectioners' sugar. Alternatively, spread with cream cheese icing.

To make cream cheese icing, beat 6 ounces of cream cheese with 4 tablespoons of softened unsalted butter until combined. Continue to beat while gradually adding 1½ cups of sifted confectioners' sugar, 1 teaspoon of finely grated lemon zest, and 2 tablespoons of lemon juice. Spread evenly over the top of the cool cake.

SERVES 8

cheese crackers.

These crispy cheese-flavored crackers are perfect served with a glass of wine or beer. They also make an excellent accompaniment to vegetable soup.

1¼ cups plain (all-purpose) flour	1 cup (4 ounces) cheddar, shredded
salt	½ cup (2 ounces) parmesan, grated
7 tablespoons unsalted butter, chilled and finely diced	

- Sift the flour and a pinch of salt into a mixing bowl. Add the butter and rub into the flour with your fingertips until the mixture resembles coarse breadcrumbs. Stir in the cheddar and parmesan. Mix well with your hands until the mixture forms a firm dough, then press into a ball. Alternatively, place in a food processor and pulse until the mixture comes together. You may need to add a little water to make the dough hold together, since cheeses and butters vary in their water content. The dough should be dry but smooth and just hold together without being sticky.

- Divide the dough into two portions. With a rolling pin, roll each portion between two sheets of baking paper to a thickness of ¼". Chill for 10–15 minutes.

- Preheat the oven to 375°F. Line an oven tray with baking paper.

- Remove the top sheet of baking paper from each piece of dough and cut the dough into shapes with a cookie cutter. Carefully transfer the shapes to the prepared oven tray. Bake for 15–20 minutes, or until pale gold. Cool on a wire rack, then store in an airtight container.

These crackers may be made without the parmesan. In this case, increase the amount of cheddar to 6 ounces.

—

The parmesan may be replaced with gruyère or another firm tasty cheese.

MAKES 24–30

cheese and chive muffins.

These cheese and chive muffins are a good savory alternative
to sweet muffins and make a tasty snack.

2½ cups all-purpose flour	⅔ cup parmesan cheese, grated
3¾ teaspoons baking powder	fresh black peppercorns
½ teaspoon baking soda	1¼ cups cheddar cheese, shredded
¼ teaspoon salt	1 cup buttermilk
2 teaspoons fresh chives, chopped	2 eggs, lightly beaten
½ cup feta cheese, cut into ¼" cubes	7 tablespoons butter, melted

- Preheat the oven to 375°F. Lightly grease a 12-cup muffin pan.

- Sift the flour, baking powder, baking soda, and salt into a mixing bowl. Stir in the chopped chives, feta cheese, parmesan, a couple of grindings of black pepper, and 1 cup of the shredded cheddar—reserve ¼ cup of the cheese to sprinkle on top. Make a well in the center of the flour mixture.

- In a separate bowl, whisk together the buttermilk, eggs, and melted butter. Pour the egg mixture into the well in the flour mixture and stir until the ingredients are just combined. Do not overmix; the batter should not be smooth.

- Divide the mixture evenly between the muffin pan. Sprinkle with the remaining cheese and bake for 25–30 minutes, or until the tops are golden and a wooden skewer inserted into the center of a muffin comes out clean. Allow to cool in the pan for 5 minutes before turning out onto a wire rack.

If you don't have any buttermilk, use 1 cup of low-fat milk that's been soured with 1 teaspoon of lemon juice. For a hint of spice, add a pinch of dry mustard to the mixture.

—

These muffins are best eaten on the day they are made and are delicious warm, spread with a little butter.

28   **SERVES 12**

cheesecake.

8 ounces plain graham crackers	1/2 cup cream
1/4 teaspoon ground ginger	2 teaspoons vanilla extract
1/2 cup unsalted butter, melted	1 teaspoon finely grated lemon zest
1 pound cream cheese	1 teaspoon lemon juice
3/4 cup sugar	confectioners' sugar, to serve
3 eggs, separated	

- Grease a 9" springform cake pan and line the base with baking paper.

- Place the graham crackers and ginger in a food processor and pulse until crushed. Add the butter and process until the mixture comes together. Using your fingertips, press the crumb mixture into the base of the tin and two-thirds of the way up the sides. Refrigerate for 30 minutes.

- Preheat the oven to 350°F.

- With an electric mixer, beat the cream cheese and sugar until creamy and well combined. Add the egg yolks, cream, vanilla, lemon zest, and juice. Beat for 2–3 minutes, or until the mixture is light and fluffy.

- Using clean beaters and a clean bowl, beat the egg whites for 3–4 minutes, or until stiff peaks form. Use a large metal spoon to gently fold the egg whites into the cream cheese mixture.

- Spoon the mixture into the prepared cake pan and smooth the top. Bake for 35–40 minutes, or until a pale golden color and just set in the center. Allow to cool, then refrigerate for 6–12 hours before serving.

- To serve, cut into slices and dust with confectioners' sugar.

SERVES 8-12

chicken curry.

This is a mildly spiced, easy-to-prepare Thai-style green curry.

1 tablespoon vegetable oil

1 small onion, finely chopped

2 cloves garlic, chopped

1 teaspoon grated fresh ginger

2–3 tablespoons Thai green curry paste

2 pounds boneless, skinless chicken breasts or thigh fillets, cut into ³/₄" pieces

¹/₃ cup coconut milk

¹/₂ pound green beans, chopped into 1¹/₂" lengths

1 tablespoon chopped cilantro

salt

- Heat the oil in a large saucepan and add the onion, garlic, and ginger. Cook over medium heat, stirring occasionally, for 3 minutes. Add the curry paste and cook, stirring, for 1 minute. Add the chicken and cook, stirring occasionally, for 2 minutes.

- Add the coconut milk and bring to a boil. Reduce the heat and simmer gently, stirring occasionally, for 30 minutes, or until the chicken is tender and no longer pink inside. The sauce should have reduced and thickened by this stage.

- Add the beans, stir well, and cook for 10 minutes, or until tender. There should not be a lot of sauce—just enough to coat the pieces of meat. If the mixture is very liquid, increase the heat and simmer until reduced. Use a spoon to remove any oil that rises to the top.

- Stir in the cilantro and season to taste with salt. Serve with steamed rice.

Vary the amount of curry paste used to suit your taste.

—

You can usually find curry paste in the international aisle of the supermarket or in East Indian or Asian food markets.

SERVES 4

chicken noodle soup.

1 medium-sized chicken

2 carrots, roughly chopped

2 onions, quartered

2 ribs celery, roughly chopped

2 bay leaves

1 tablespoon vegetable oil

1 leek, sliced

1 clove garlic, chopped

2 carrots, extra, sliced

1 onion, extra, sliced

1 rib celery, extra, sliced

3½ ounces dried fine egg noodles

½ teaspoon grated fresh ginger

salt and freshly ground black pepper

2 tablespoons chopped flat-leaf parsley or cilantro

2 scallions, finely sliced

■ Place the chicken, carrots, onions, celery, and bay leaves in a large saucepan or stockpot. Add 8 cups of water, or enough to cover the chicken and vegetables. Bring to a boil. Remove any foam from the broth and simmer for 1 hour.

■ Remove the chicken and set aside to cool slightly.

■ Strain the broth, discarding the solids.

■ Heat the oil in a large saucepan over medium heat. Add the leek, garlic, and extra carrots, onion, and celery, and cook, stirring occasionally, for 5 minutes, or until tender. Add the strained broth and bring to a boil. Reduce the heat and simmer for 10 minutes.

■ Meanwhile, strip the chicken meat from the bones and tear into bite-sized pieces. Add to the soup.

■ Add the noodles and ginger and simmer for 4–5 minutes, or until the noodles are soft. Season to taste with salt and freshly ground black pepper. Ladle into bowls and top with parsley and scallions.

SERVES 4

chicken pie.

1 medium-sized chicken	2 tablespoons plain (all-purpose) flour
2 onions, quartered	1 tablespoon chopped chives or parsley
2 carrots, chopped	
1 bay leaf	salt and freshly ground black pepper
1 tablespoon olive oil	1 egg, beaten
2 leeks, sliced	1 12-ounce package frozen puff pastry, thawed
4 tablespoons unsalted butter	

- Place the chicken, onions, carrots, and bay leaf in a large saucepan. Cover with cold water and bring to a boil. Skim off any fat, reduce the heat and simmer for 1 hour.

- Remove the chicken from the broth and set aside to cool. Strain the broth, discard the solids, and return the strained liquid to the saucepan. Boil rapidly until it has reduced to about 2 cups. Set aside.

- Remove the meat from the chicken, cut into bite-sized pieces and place in a bowl.

- Heat the oil in a frying pan over medium heat. Add the leeks and cook, stirring, for 4–5 minutes, or until tender. Transfer to the bowl containing the chicken meat.

- Melt the butter in a small saucepan over medium heat. Stir in the flour and cook for 1 minute. Whisk in the reserved stock. Bring to a boil and continue to whisk until thickened and smooth. Stir in the chives and season well with salt and freshly ground black pepper.

- Add enough of the sauce to the leek and chicken mixture to moisten it. Allow to cool.

- Preheat the oven to 375°F.

- Spoon the mixture into a large pie dish and insert a pie funnel (if using). Roll out the pastry to a size large enough to cover the pie. Place over the pie, pressing down on the edges to seal. Trim away any excess pastry and use to decorate the top of the pie. Brush the pastry with the beaten egg and bake for 40–45 minutes, or until the pastry is golden and has risen.

SERVES 4-6

chicken, roasted.

1 medium-sized chicken	salt and freshly ground black pepper
1 lemon, halved	½ cup white wine
5 cloves garlic, unpeeled	1½ cups chicken stock (see page 39) or water
1 tablespoon olive oil	

- Preheat the oven to 400°F.

- Rinse the chicken and pat dry with kitchen paper. Place in a roasting pan, breast-side up, and squeeze the juice of half a lemon over the bird. Place the other lemon half inside the cavity, along with one of the garlic cloves. Scatter the remaining garlic in the pan.

- Drizzle the oil over the breast of the chicken. Sprinkle generously with salt and freshly ground black pepper.

- Roast for 65–70 minutes, basting the bird with the pan juices every 20 minutes. To test if the chicken is cooked, insert a sharp knife or metal skewer into the thigh cavity—the juice should run clear.

- Transfer the roasted chicken to a serving dish and allow to rest for 10 minutes. Warm the serving plates in the oven for 2–3 minutes.

- To make a sauce, pour off the fat from the roasting pan. Place the roasting pan over medium heat on the stove top and add the wine and chicken stock. Stir well with a wooden spoon and scrape any bits stuck to the bottom of the pan, incorporating them into the sauce. Bring to a boil and simmer until the sauce is reduced and slightly thickened.

- Season to taste with salt and freshly ground black pepper. Alternatively, make a gravy by following the directions on page 91.

Use a free-range, chemical-free chicken if available.

———

A medium-sized chicken (3-3¼ pounds) will feed four people.

SERVES 4

chicken stew.

4 pounds cut-up broiler-fryer chicken	2 cloves garlic, crushed
4 tablespoons flour	2 cups white wine
4 tablespoons olive oil	2 cups chicken stock
5 slices bacon or pancetta, roughly chopped	1 bay leaf
	1½ cups frozen peas, thawed
12 pearl onions, peeled	salt and freshly ground black pepper
2 leeks, sliced	2 tablespoons parsley, chopped

- Preheat the oven to 350°F. In a shallow bowl, lightly dust the chicken pieces in flour.

- Heat half of the oil in a large frying pan over medium heat. Season the chicken with salt and pepper and cook in batches, adding a little extra oil if needed, until browned. Be careful not to overcrowd the frying pan, as the meat will then steam rather than sear. Transfer to a large casserole dish.

- Heat the remaining oil in the frying pan over medium heat. Add the bacon, onions, leeks, and garlic and cook, stirring occasionally, for 7–10 minutes, or until the vegetables are tender, and the onions are lightly colored. Transfer to the casserole dish.

- Place the frying pan back on the heat and add the white wine, stirring with a wooden spoon to remove any bits stuck to the bottom. Pour over the chicken. Again, place the frying pan back on the heat and add the stock and bay leaf. Bring to a boil; pour over the chicken. Cover the casserole dish and transfer to the oven. Cook for 1 hour, stirring occasionally.

- Remove the stew from the oven and stir in the peas, return to the oven and cook for 15 minutes longer. If you want to thicken the sauce a little, remove the chicken pieces to a warm spot and reduce the liquid by boiling over high heat. Season to taste. Serve chicken and sauce garnished with chopped parsley.

This is a good dish to make ahead of time. Simply reheat the casserole in a large saucepan on the stove and serve.

SERVES 4-6

chicken stock.

Chicken stock is a great base for soups, risottos, and sauces,
and making your own is simple.

3 pounds chicken bones (wings, necks,
and giblets are good)

2 unpeeled onions, quartered

2 carrots, chopped

2 ribs celery, roughly chopped

1 teaspoon black peppercorns

3 bay leaves

6–8 parsley stalks

4 sprigs thyme

- Place the chicken bones in a large stockpot. Add the remainder of the ingredients and enough cold water to cover by 2". Bring to a boil, reduce the heat to low and simmer gently for 3–4 hours. Be careful not to let the mixture boil, otherwise the stock will become cloudy. Skim the surface with a spoon to remove any foam.

- Strain the stock and discard the solids. Allow the liquid to cool, then refrigerate overnight.

- The next day, skim off any fat that has solidified on the top. Refrigerate for 2–3 days, or freeze in 2-cup containers for up to 3 months.

*Use the bones left after your next roast chicken, boosted with a few wings
or giblets, to make a perfectly good stock.*

—

Try using other vegetables in the stock, such as mushroom trimmings and/or leeks.

—

Be careful not to add too many carrots, as they can make the stock very sweet.

—

*Leaving the onion skins on gives the stock good color. If you want
a paler broth, remove the skins.*

MAKES 8 CUPS

chocolate brownies.

4 ounces dark chocolate, roughly chopped

½ cup unsalted butter, cubed

4 eggs

1½ cups sugar

1 teaspoon vanilla extract

1 cup plain (all-purpose) flour, sifted

1 cup pecans or walnuts, lightly toasted and roughly chopped

- Preheat the oven to 325°F. Grease an 8" × 12" baking pan and line the base and sides with baking paper.

- Melt the chocolate and butter in a heatproof bowl set over a saucepan of hot water, stirring occasionally, until smooth. Allow to cool.

- In a large bowl with an electric mixer, beat the eggs, sugar, and vanilla for 3–4 minutes, or until pale and fluffy. Beat in the cooled chocolate mixture. Add the flour and beat until smooth. Stir in the nuts.

- Spoon the mixture into the prepared baking pan and smooth the surface. Bake for 30 minutes, or until dark brown and the top has formed a crust. Allow to cool in the pan. Remove and cut into squares. Dust with confectioners' sugar to serve.

To make orange and macadamia brownies, omit the pecans or walnuts and stir into the mixture 2 teaspoons of finely grated orange zest and 3½ ounces of roughly chopped macadamia nuts.

—

Brownies can be drizzled with melted chocolate or spread with chocolate icing, or frosting (see page 42).

MAKES 24

chocolate cake.

This dark, fudgey, and delicious chocolate cake is easy to make. It is perfect for afternoon tea or coffee, and packs well for lunch boxes or a picnic.

8 ounces dark chocolate, roughly chopped

1 cup unsalted butter, cubed

1 teaspoon instant coffee powder

1 cup plain (all-purpose) flour, sifted

1½ teaspoons baking powder

⅛ teaspoon salt

4 eggs, beaten

½ cup sugar

½ cup ground hazelnuts

- Preheat the oven to 325°F. Grease an 8" springform cake pan and line the base with baking paper.

- Melt the chocolate, butter, and coffee powder in a heatproof bowl set over a saucepan of hot water, stirring occasionally, until smooth. Allow to cool.

- In a small mixing bowl, combine the flour, baking powder, and salt.

- In a large bowl with an electric mixer, beat the eggs and sugar for 4–5 minutes, or until pale and fluffy. Beat in the cooled chocolate mixture until smooth. Gently fold in the flour mixture and hazelnuts.

- Pour the mixture into the prepared pan and bake for 50–55 minutes, or until a wooden skewer inserted into the center comes out clean. Leave to cool in the pan for 10 minutes before turning out. Allow to cool completely on a wire rack before serving lightly dusted with confectioners' sugar.

The chocolate and butter can be melted in a microwave on medium for 1–2 minutes. Stir until smooth.

—

Replace the ground hazelnuts with ground almonds, if you prefer.

—

Make a simple icing (frosting) by melting 4 ounces of roughly chopped dark chocolate and 2½ tablespoons of cubed unsalted butter. Stir until smooth. Allow to cool. Beat with a wooden spoon until fluffy, then spread over the cooled cake.

SERVES 8

chocolate cake (flourless).

8 ounces dark chocolate,
roughly chopped

²/₃ cup sugar

½ cup plus 2 tablespoons unsalted
butter, cubed

1 tablespoon brandy

1 tablespoon strong black coffee

1 cup ground almonds or hazelnuts

5 eggs, separated

- Preheat the oven to 350°F. Grease a 9" springform cake pan and line the base with baking paper.

- Melt the chocolate, sugar, butter, brandy, and coffee in a heatproof bowl over a saucepan of hot water, stirring occasionally until smooth.

- Transfer to a large bowl and stir in the ground nuts. Add the egg yolks, one at a time, beating well after each addition.

- In a separate clean bowl, whisk the egg whites until they form medium-firm peaks. Stir a third of the whites into the chocolate mixture to slacken it, then gently fold through the remaining whites with a large metal spoon or spatula.

- Pour the mixture into the prepared pan and bake for 45–50 minutes, or until the cake is firm to the touch but still a little soft in the center.

- Allow to cool completely in the pan. The cake will sink a little as it cools. Carefully remove from the pan and serve lightly dusted with confectioners' sugar.

SERVES 8-10

chocolate chip cookies.

³/₄ cup plain (all-purpose flour), sifted

½ teaspoon baking soda

pinch of salt

½ cup butter, softened at room temperature

½ cup sugar

½ teaspoon vanilla extract

1 large egg, lightly beaten

½ cup dark chocolate chips

2½ ounces chopped pecans

- Preheat the oven to 375°F. Line two cookie sheets with baking paper.

- In a small bowl, combine the flour, baking soda and salt. Set aside.

- In another bowl, with an electric mixer, beat the butter, sugar, and vanilla for 2–3 minutes, or until soft and well mixed.

- Add the beaten egg and a tablespoonful of the flour mixture, adding one tablespoon at a time, mixing well after each addition. Continue to mix to form a stiff batter.

- Drop the batter mixture by heaping tablespoons about 2" apart onto the cookie sheets.

- Bake for 8–10 minutes until the cookie is firm to the touch. Cool on a wire rack and store in an airtight container.

MAKES ABOUT 30

chocolate cookies.

With chocolate, as with everything else in cooking, the better the quality
of the raw ingredient, the better the end result.

4 ounces dark chocolate,
roughly chopped

$1/4$ cup unsalted butter, chopped

1 egg

1 cup lightly packed brown sugar

$1^1/_4$ cups plain (all-purpose) flour, sifted

$1^3/_4$ teaspoons baking powder

$1/_8$ teaspoon salt

- Preheat the oven to 350°F. Line two oven trays with baking paper.

- Melt the chocolate and butter in a heatproof bowl set over a saucepan of hot water, stirring occasionally, until smooth.

- In a separate bowl, beat the egg and brown sugar with a wooden spoon until combined.

- Stir the chocolate mixture into the egg mixture. Add the flour, baking powder, and salt and mix until smooth and thick. Refrigerate for 20 minutes.

- Roll teaspoonfuls of the dough into balls and place on the oven trays, allowing 2" between each for the cookies to spread while baking.

- Bake for 7–10 minutes, or until the cookies are firm to the touch and the tops have wrinkled slightly. Cool on a wire rack and store in an airtight container.

As an indulgence, add 1 cup of chocolate chips to the mixture for a dense, rich treat.

—

To decorate, these cookies may be spread, dipped, or drizzled with melted dark, milk, or white chocolate.

MAKES 24-30

chocolate mousse.

Universally adored and made with just three ingredients, chocolate mousse is equally at home at a dinner party or a simple supper.

3 eggs, separated	**¾ cup cream**
6½ ounces dark chocolate, roughly chopped	

- In a small bowl, lightly beat the egg yolks.

- Melt the chocolate in a heatproof bowl set over a saucepan of hot water, stirring occasionally, until smooth. Remove from the heat and gradually add the beaten yolks, mixing until smooth. Fold through the cream and stir until combined.

- Beat the egg whites with an electric mixer until soft peaks form. Fold a little of the whites into the mousse to slacken it, then gently fold through the remaining whites. Mix until there are no streaks or pockets of egg white.

- Cook over low heat for about 5 minutes, stirring constantly. Do not boil.

- Pour the mixture evenly into six small ramekins or cups, cover with plastic wrap and chill for at least 3 hours, or until firm.

Add to the mixture 2 tablespoons of strong espresso and a little brandy or liqueur for greater depth of flavor.

—

Chocolate mousse can be made ahead of time and kept covered in the fridge for 2–3 days.

SERVES 6

chocolate puddings.

This is a simple, quick, and easy dessert. As the puddings cook,
the batter turns magically into a rich chocolate sauce, topped with
a soft chocolate sponge.

1 cup plain (all-purpose) flour	½ cup milk
1½ teaspoons baking powder	1 egg, lightly beaten
¼ teaspoon salt	4 tablespoons unsalted butter, melted
⅓ cup cocoa	½ teaspoon vanilla extract
½ cup sugar	½ cup lightly packed brown sugar

- Preheat the oven to 350°F. Grease four 1-cup-capacity ramekins or small pudding bowls.

- In a mixing bowl, sift together the flour, baking powder, salt, and half the cocoa. Stir in the sugar and make a well in the center.

- In a separate bowl, combine the milk, egg, melted butter, and vanilla. Pour into the well in the dry mixture and mix until smooth.

- Spoon the mixture into the prepared ramekins and place on an oven tray. Combine the brown sugar and the remaining cocoa and sprinkle evenly over the top of each pudding. Bring 1 cup of water to a boil and carefully pour enough of the boiling water over the back of a spoon to fill each pudding to three-quarters. Bake for 20–25 minutes, or until the puddings have risen and are firm to the touch. Serve immediately, lightly dusted with confectioners' sugar.

These puddings are delicious served with thick cream or good-quality vanilla ice cream.
One large pudding can be made in a 4-cup capacity soufflé dish.
In this case, bake for 40–50 minutes.

SERVES 4

chocolate sauce.

This easy-to-make, all-time favorite sauce is fantastic served warm
over ice cream, pancakes, waffles, poached fruit, or puddings.

8 ounces dark chocolate,
roughly chopped

¾ cup cream

2½ tablespoons unsalted butter

1 tablespoon honey or golden syrup

■ Place all of the ingredients in a small saucepan over low heat. Stir until the chocolate has
melted and the sauce is smooth.

*Chocolate sauce is delicious flavored with a little alcohol. Add 1 tablespoon of brandy
or liqueur at the end of the cooking time and remove from the heat.*

—

*Any excess sauce may be stored in the fridge for up to 1 week.
Gently reheat before serving.*

MAKES 2 CUPS

chocolate truffles.

Chocolate truffles are the ultimate in chocolate treats, and this rich, elegant, and highly treasured confectionery is easy to make.

½ cup cream	1 tablespoon cognac or brandy
8 ounces dark chocolate, roughly chopped	cocoa, to coat
2½ tablespoons unsalted butter, cubed	

- Heat the cream in a small saucepan and gently bring to a boil. Remove from the heat and add the chocolate and butter. Mix with a spoon or whisk until smooth. Add the cognac or brandy and stir well until combined. Cover and refrigerate until firm.

- Using a melon-baller or two teaspoons, shape the mixture into balls ¾" in diameter. Roll each ball between the palms of your hands to smooth them out. If the weather is humid and this is difficult to do, roll them into rough shapes, freeze for 10 minutes and reroll.

- Coat the truffles by tossing in cocoa. The truffles are best eaten fresh, but will keep in an airtight container in the refrigerator for up to 2 weeks.

Be sure to use the best-quality chocolate you can find. It really makes a difference. Try rolling the truffles in finely chopped hazelnuts, macadamia nuts, or almonds instead of cocoa.

—

Vary the flavor by replacing the cognac with Cointreau, Grand Marnier, or cherry-flavored brandy.

MAKES 20

cinnamon toast.

½ cup sugar
2 teaspoons ground cinnamon

6 slices white bread
4 tablespoons unsalted butter, softened

- In a small bowl, combine the sugar and cinnamon.

- Preheat the broiler.

- Toast the bread lightly on both sides, then butter each slice, spreading the butter right to the edges. Using a shaker or spoon, sprinkle each slice of toast evenly with plenty of the cinnamon–sugar mixture.

- Return the slices to the broiler and toast until the sugar starts to melt. Remove, trim away the crusts and cut into quarters. Serve hot.

Any unused cinnamon and sugar mixture can be stored in a screw-top jar.

—

For a change of pace, try using whole wheat or whole-grain bread for a chewier texture.

SERVES 3-4

coleslaw.

½ Savoy cabbage or red cabbage, finely shredded

2 carrots, coarsely grated

1 red onion, finely sliced

1 clove garlic, finely chopped

3 scallions, finely sliced

1 tablespoon olive oil

1 tablespoon lemon juice

salt and freshly ground black pepper

½ cup mayonnaise (see page 106)

- Mix together the cabbage, carrot, onion, garlic, scallions, oil, and lemon juice. Season to taste with salt and freshly ground black pepper. Mix in the mayonnaise. Add a little extra mayonnaise if necessary to coat the cabbage evenly.

- Coleslaw can be made 2–3 hours ahead of time. Simply cover and chill until needed.

One to two tablespoons of plain yogurt or sour cream is delicious added to the mayonnaise before mixing into the coleslaw.

—

To make an Asian-style coleslaw, add 1 seeded and chopped large red chili, 2 tablespoons of finely chopped mint, and 1 cup of bean sprouts to the salad. Omit the mayonnaise and make a dressing by thoroughly combining 1 tablespoon of Thai fish sauce, 2 tablespoons of lime juice, 2 teaspoons of soy sauce, 1 teaspoon of brown sugar, and 1 tablespoon of olive oil. Pour the dressing over the salad and set aside for 10 minutes to allow the flavors to develop before serving.

—

Look for Thai fish sauce in the international aisle of supermarkets.

SERVES 4-6

corn and chicken chowder.

7 cups chicken stock

3 cobs sweet corn, husks removed

1 tablespoon corn flour

¾ cup cream

2 tablespoons dry sherry

2 boneless, skinless chicken breasts, finely chopped or cubed

3 scallions, chopped

- In a large saucepan, bring the chicken stock to a boil and add the corn cobs. Simmer for 8–10 minutes or until the corn is tender.

- Remove the corn from the saucepan, leaving the cooking water in the pan. Cool the corn until comfortable enough to handle with your hands, then using a sharp knife, cut the kernels from the cobs, putting half the kernels back into the saucepan with the reserved cooking liquid.

- Place the remaining kernels, corn flour, and cream into a food processor and puree until smooth, then transfer the puree to the saucepan. Bring the mixture to a gentle simmer over medium heat, stirring frequently.

- Add the sherry and chicken to the saucepan. Continue to simmer for 8–10 minutes until the chicken is cooked and no longer pink in the center.

- Season to taste with salt and freshly ground black pepper. Serve garnished with chopped scallions.

For a slightly different flavor, add a dash of soy sauce to the soup just before serving or try a drizzle of sesame oil in each bowl.

SERVES 4

corn bread.

1 cup plain (all-purpose) flour	1 egg
1 cup fine corn meal	1 tablespoon sugar
2 teaspoons baking powder	¼ cup vegetable oil
1 teaspoon salt	1 tablespoon chopped fresh sage
1 cup milk	

- Preheat the oven to 425°F. Lightly oil and then flour an 8" shallow square cake pan.

- In a medium mixing bowl combine the flour, corn meal, baking powder, and salt. In another bowl whisk together the milk, egg, sugar, oil, and sage. Add the wet ingredients to the dry ingredients and stir until just combined.

- Place the prepared pan in the oven for 2–3 minutes to heat.

- Pour the batter into the pan and bake in the top half of the oven for 20–25 minutes, or until firm and golden brown on top. A wooden skewer inserted into the middle should come out clean.

- Remove from the oven and leave to cool for 10 minutes; then remove the cake from the pan and continue to cool completely on a wire rack. Cut into squares to serve.

For a hint of spice, try adding finely chopped fresh green or red chilies to the mixture before baking or for a hearty texture, add ½ cup of grated cheddar cheese.

—

This recipe can also be made in a 12-cup muffin pan. Spoon the mixture into hot, greased, and floured muffin cups and bake in the top half of the oven for 15 minutes.

SERVES 12

corn bread stuffing.

⅓ corn bread recipe, prepared (see page 55)

1 tablespoon vegetable oil

5 slices smoked bacon, chopped in 1" pieces

1 small onion, finely chopped

2 ribs celery, chopped

1 red pepper, seeds removed and finely chopped

1 clove garlic, crushed

1 tablespoon lemon zest

1 lemon, juiced

2 tablespoons chopped fresh sage

1 tablespoon chopped fresh chives

1 egg, lightly beaten

- Crumble the prepared corn bread into a large mixing bowl.

- Heat the oil in a frying pan over medium heat. Add the bacon and cook, stirring occasionally for 2 minutes. Add the onion, celery, pepper, and garlic and sauté for 4–5 minutes, or until the vegetables have softened.

- Transfer to the bowl with the cornbread. Stir in the lemon zest, juice, sage, and chives. Add the beaten egg and mix until combined. The mixture should be crumbly and just come together in clumps. Drizzle with a little extra oil if needed. Season well and bake until done.

This recipe can be used to stuff a large chicken, or if you prefer, try wrapping the corn bread in foil, roll into a sausage shape, and bake alongside the chicken.

—

To stuff a turkey, double the corn bread mixture.

SERVES 4

corn cakes (corn fritters).

2 cups whole corn, fresh or frozen	black peppercorns
¾ cup plain (all purpose flour)	⅓ cup milk
½ teaspoon baking powder	1 large egg, beaten
½ teaspoon baking soda	¼ cup lemon juice
½ teaspoon salt	vegetable oil, for frying

- Place the corn kernels into a large bowl. Sift in the flour, baking powder, baking soda, salt, and a few grindings of freshly ground black pepper.

- Add the milk, beaten egg, and lemon juice and stir into the flour and corn mixture; mixing until just combined. The batter should fall off the spoon with a light tap. Add a little extra milk if necessary.

- Add enough oil to cover the base of a large heavy frying pan. Heat over medium heat— the oil is ready for frying when a cube of bread turns golden in 30 seconds.

- Add 3–4 large spoonfuls of the batter to the frying pan and cook each side for about 3 minutes, or until golden brown. The corn cakes will raise a little as they cook, don't be tempted to press them down.

- Repeat with the remaining mixture, keeping the cooked corn cakes on a warm platter or in warming tray until ready to serve.

For a sweet touch, top the fritters with your favorite flavor of jam or serve plain with a side of bacon and grilled tomatoes.

SERVES 4

corn on the cob.

This is the true taste of summer. Whether you boil or barbecue your corn on the cob, make sure you eat it with lots of butter, sea salt, and freshly ground black pepper. You are definitely supposed to get messy when eating corn on the cob!

■ To boil corn on the cob, discard the husk and silk from the cob and place the cob in a large saucepan of unsalted boiling water. Add 1 tablespoon of olive oil and boil for 8–10 minutes, or until a kernel can be pried easily from a cob with the point of a knife. The kernels should be tender but slightly chewy, with a juicy, sweet flavor.

■ To grill or roast corn on the cob, strip back the husk, remove the silk, brush the corn with melted butter or oil and rewrap the corn in the husk. Tie the husk back into position with string, or tightly twist the husk ends together to secure. Soak in a bowl of water for 10 minutes. Grill for 15 minutes on a hot barbecue or preheated grill plate, or roast in a preheated 425°F oven for 15–20 minutes, turning every 5 minutes.

Corn on the cob is delicious served with herb butter (see page 160) or garlic butter (see page 83).

—

The recipe above works well using one corn on the cob or a dozen. Experiment and see which method you like best.

couscous.

Couscous is the perfect healthy convenience food and is used in salads, as well as to accompany tagines or braised dishes. Most varieties available are precooked and only need moistening and steaming, so preparation time is minimal.

1 cup couscous	2 tablespoons butter or vegetable oil
1¼ cups chicken stock (see page 39) or water	salt

- Place the couscous in a medium-sized heatproof bowl and pour the stock or boiling water over the couscous. Add the butter or oil and a pinch of salt. Cover with plastic wrap and stand for 5 minutes, or until the liquid has been absorbed.

- If using in a salad or serving at room temperature, simply fluff the grains with a fork. If serving hot as an accompaniment to a braised dish or tagine, place the bowl containing the couscous over a saucepan of simmering water for 5–10 minutes, or until warmed through. Fluff with a fork to help separate the grains.

Traditionally, couscous is placed in a steamer lined with muslin or cheesecloth and heated over simmering water for 5–10 minutes to warm through.

—

Chopped mint, cilantro, or flat-leaf parsley may be folded through couscous before serving.

—

Make a delicious couscous salad by adding in roasted pumpkin, shredded arugula or basil, finely grated lemon zest, chopped red onion, crushed garlic, chopped fresh chili, salt and pepper, and a drizzle of olive oil.

SERVES 4

crab cakes.

1 pound fresh crabmeat

2¼ cups fresh breadcrumbs

3 tablespoons mayonnaise

2 tablespoons chives, finely chopped

1 teaspoon Dijon-style mustard

1 small egg, lightly beaten

dash of Tabasco sauce

½ cup plain flour, to dust

vegetable oil, for frying

fresh lemon wedges, to serve

- Place the crabmeat in a bowl and break up the meat with a fork. Add the bread crumbs, mayonnaise, chives, mustard, and beaten egg. Mix with a fork until thoroughly combined. Season the mixture with salt and freshly ground black pepper. Add the Tabasco sauce (crab cakes are good with a little spice, but don't over do it).

- Place the flour in a shallow dish (adding more if needed). Shape the crab mixture into eight patties and then roll each in the flour to give them a light dusting. Transfer the patties to a plate lined with baking parchment, cover with plastic wrap and refrigerate for at least 30 minutes to firm up a little.

- In a heavy frying pan, coat the bottom of the pan with ½" of oil. Heat the pan over medium heat. The oil will be hot enough when a cube of bread browns in 30 seconds. Cook the crab cakes for 4–5 minutes on each side, or until golden brown (you may have to do this in batches). Serve hot with a dressed salad and fresh lemon wedges.

Fresh bread crumbs are easily made at home, simply remove the crusts from 3–4 thick slices of bread, break the slices into pieces and then whiz in a food processor until fine.

—

The best crab cakes are made using fresh crab meat, but they can also be made with good quality canned crab. Be sure to drain the crab meat before using.

SERVES 4

crackers.

2 cups plain (all purpose) flour	black peppercorns
1 teaspoon baking powder	2 tablespoons sesame seeds
½ teaspoon salt	¼ cup butter, chilled and diced
2 tablespoons poppy seeds	

- Preheat the oven to 350°F. Line two cookie sheets with baking paper.

- Sift the flour, baking powder, and salt into a mixing bowl. Mix in the seeds and a couple grindings of black pepper. Add the butter to the bowl and, using your fingertips, rub the butter into the flour until the mixture looks like coarse breadcrumbs.

- Make a well in the center of the flour and pour in ½ cup of iced water. Mix with a large metal spoon until the mixture comes together. Pat the mixture into a ball and flatten slightly. Cover with plastic wrap and chill for 30 minutes.

- Divide the dough into two portions. Roll out each portion between two sheets of baking paper to a thickness of 1/8". Cut the dough into rounds with a 2½" round cookie cutter.

- Repeat with the remaining portion of dough. Try not to knead the dough too much; shape any scraps of dough into a ball and gently reroll.

- Place the crackers onto the prepared cookie sheets and bake for 20 minutes, or until golden. Cool on a wire rack. Store the crackers in an air-tight container for up to 5 days.

MAKES 18-24 CRACKERS

cranberry sauce.

Cranberry sauce is wonderful with turkey or ham, in sandwiches, or served simply with cheese.

1 pound fresh or frozen and thawed cranberries
½ cup orange juice
2 teaspoons finely grated orange zest

⅓ cup wine such as port
1 cinnamon stick
1–1½ cups sugar

- Place the cranberries, orange juice and zest, wine, and cinnamon stick in a medium-sized stainless-steel saucepan and slowly bring to a boil over low heat. Simmer gently, stirring occasionally, for 10–15 minutes, or until the cranberries have burst and the sauce has reduced slightly.

- Add the sugar and stir until dissolved. Cranberries can be quite tart; taste and add a little extra sugar if needed. Discard the cinnamon stick. Transfer the mixture to a bowl and allow to cool. The sauce will thicken slightly. Serve cold.

The wine may be replaced with water or extra orange juice, if you prefer.

—

Other spices work well with cranberry sauce. One whole star anise used in place of the cinnamon stick makes an interesting variation.

MAKES 2 CUPS

crème anglaise.

2½ cups milk	6 egg yolks
1 vanilla bean	½ cup sugar

- Pour the milk into a small saucepan. Using a sharp knife, split the vanilla bean in half lengthways. Scrape out the seeds and add the pod and the seeds to the saucepan of milk. Bring the mixture to a simmer over low heat.

- In a large mixing bowl, whisk together the egg yolks and sugar for 4–5 minutes, or until the sugar has dissolved and the mixture is thick and pale. Gently whisk the hot milk mixture, including the vanilla bean pod, into the yolk mixture. Return this mixture to the saucepan and cook over low heat, stirring constantly with a wooden spoon, until the mixture thickens slightly to form a custard that coats the back of the spoon. Do not allow the mixture to boil or it will curdle. Remove from the heat and strain into a bowl, discarding the vanilla bean pod.

- Serve warm or at room temperature with puddings, fruit pies, or poached or fresh fruit. Crème anglaise can be stored in an airtight container in the fridge for up to 5 days. Simply bring to room temperature before use.

A richer version can be made by replacing the milk with half milk and half cream.

—

Brandy crème anglaise can be made by adding 2 tablespoons of brandy to the mixture after removing from the heat.

MAKES 3 CUPS

cupcakes.

1½ cups plain (all-purpose) flour	¾ cup sugar
2¼ teaspoons baking powder	1 teaspoon vanilla extract
¼ teaspoon salt	2 eggs, beaten
½ cup unsalted butter, softened	½ cup milk

- Preheat the oven to 350°F. Line a 12-cup muffin pan with paper baking cups.

- Sift the flour into a large mixing bowl. Add the remaining ingredients and beat with an electric mixer on low speed for 2 minutes, or until combined. Increase the speed to medium and beat for 3 minutes, or until pale and smooth.

- Spoon the mixture evenly into the baking cups. Bake for 15–20 minutes, or until golden and firm to the touch. A wooden skewer inserted into the center of a cupcake should come out clean. Cool on a wire rack. Ice and decorate as desired.

For orange cupcakes, substitute ½ cup of freshly squeezed orange juice for the milk and add 1 tablespoon of finely grated orange zest to the cake batter. Bake as above.

—

To make lemon icing (frosting), combine 1 cup of sifted confectioners' sugar, 2 tablespoons of softened unsalted butter and 1–2 tablespoons of lemon juice. Beat until smooth and spread over the cupcakes.

—

To make strawberry icing (frosting), mash 6 large ripe strawberries with a fork. Combine the strawberries, 1 cup of sifted confectioners' sugar, 1–2 drops of pink food coloring and 1–2 tablespoons of lemon juice. Beat until smooth and spread over the cupcakes.

MAKES 12

eggplant dip.

2 large eggplants
3-4 cloves garlic, chopped
2 tablespoons lemon juice

1 tablespoon olive oil
salt and freshly ground black pepper
paprika, to serve

- Preheat the oven to 350°F.

- Pierce the eggplants a few times with a metal skewer. Place in a baking pan and bake for 40 minutes, or until tender. Allow to cool.

- Cut the eggplants in half lengthways and scoop out the flesh. Place the flesh in a fine sieve and allow to drain for 20 minutes.

- Transfer the eggplant flesh to a food processor or blender. Add the garlic, lemon juice, and oil and purée until smooth. Season to taste with salt and freshly ground black pepper. Add a little extra lemon juice or oil if the mixture is very thick.

- Serve in a bowl sprinkled with paprika. This dip can be stored in an airtight container in the refrigerator for 2–3 days.

MAKES 2 CUPS

eggs, baked.

This is good as a breakfast dish, or delicious served as a light lunch
with a green salad.

½ cup cream	4 large free-range eggs
1 tablespoon chopped chives	salt and freshly ground black pepper

■ Preheat the oven to 350°F. Lightly grease four 6-ounce ramekins, soufflé dishes, or ovenproof cups.

■ In a small bowl, combine the cream and the chives. Pour equal quantities of the mixture into the four ramekins. Break an egg into each ramekin. Season with salt and freshly ground black pepper.

■ Place the ramekins in a baking pan and fill the pan with enough boiling water to come one-third up the sides of the ramekins. Carefully transfer to the oven and bake for 8–10 minutes, or until the eggs are set to your liking. These eggs are delicious served with fingers of toasted pita bread or brioche.

Baked eggs lend themselves to all sorts of variations. Fresh crabmeat added to the cream mixture is good, as is chopped smoked salmon.

—

Tarragon, chervil, or parsley can be substituted for the chives, if you prefer.

SERVES 4

eggs, boiled.

A boiled egg with toast "soldiers" is the perfect breakfast. Not only is it compact and nutritious, it's also a great excuse to get the egg cups out of the cupboard. A boiled egg is also a great dish to have for supper if you have had a little too much to eat for Sunday lunch. The cooking time is crucial here—an extra minute on the boil can make a big difference.

4 eggs	**toast, buttered and cut into fingers, to serve**
salt and freshly ground black pepper	

- Place the eggs in a small saucepan and cover with cold water. Bring to a boil over medium heat. Reduce the heat and simmer for 3 minutes for soft, runny eggs, 4 minutes for a firmer set, or 5 minutes for hard-boiled.

- Remove the eggs with a slotted spoon and transfer to egg cups. Use a knife to slice off the tops.

- Serve with salt and freshly ground black pepper and buttered fingers of freshly toasted bread. Boiled eggs are also delicious served with seasoned salt or zahtar, a Middle-Eastern herb mix, on the side.

To make seasoned salt, combine 2 teaspoons of sea salt, ½ teaspoon of freshly ground black pepper, ¼ teaspoon of ground coriander, and a pinch of chili powder.

—

To make zahtar, combine 2 teaspoons of sea salt, 1 teaspoon of sesame seeds, ¼ teaspoon of ground cumin, and ½ teaspoon of dried thyme.

SERVES 2

eggs, poached.

salt	4 fresh eggs
white wine vinegar	

- Half-fill a deep frying pan or wide saucepan with water. Add a teaspoon of salt and a dash of white vinegar. Bring the water to a gentle boil.

- Carefully break one egg into a small, shallow dish or saucer and gently slide the egg into the simmering water. Repeat with the remaining eggs.

- Lower the heat until the water is barely moving, allowing the eggs to cook gently without breaking. Cook for 4–5 minutes, or until the whites are set. Remove the eggs with a slotted spoon and drain.

The most successful poached eggs are made from very fresh eggs.

—

If the white separates from the yolk, it means the egg was not fresh, or that the water was not simmering sufficiently when the egg was added.

—

Only cook four eggs at a time in one frying pan or saucepan.

SERVES 4

eggs, scrambled.

To make perfect scrambled eggs, you need to cook the eggs
very slowly. The best way to achieve this is to cook them in a bowl
placed over a saucepan of simmering water. This method takes longer,
but the result is worth the effort.

6 eggs	**salt and freshly ground black pepper**
1 tablespoon cream	**1 tablespoon butter**

- Gently whisk the eggs with the cream and a pinch of salt and freshly ground black pepper in a small heatproof mixing bowl.

- Place the bowl over a saucepan of gently simmering water, making sure the bottom of the bowl does not touch the water. Cook, turning the mixture occasionally with a large metal spoon, until the egg thickens. As the egg thickens and begins to scramble, add the butter. Season to taste with more salt and freshly ground black pepper. Serve on hot, buttered toast.

Chopped chives or chervil are delicious folded into the mixture just before serving.

—

Dress up scrambled eggs with some smoked salmon and a glass of bubbly on the side.

SERVES 2

fish cakes.

450 g (14 oz) potatoes, peeled and cut into chunks

650 g (1 lb 5 oz) cooked fish fillets, flaked

6 spring onions (scallions), finely chopped

2 tablespoons chopped flat-leaf parsley or basil

finely grated zest of 1 lemon

1 tablespoon lemon juice

½ teaspoon English mustard

1 egg yolk

salt and freshly ground black pepper

1 cup plain (all-purpose) flour

1 egg, beaten

½ cup milk

1 cup dry breadcrumbs

¼ cup olive oil

- Place the potato pieces in a large saucepan of salted water. Bring to the boil and cook for 20–25 minutes, or until tender. Drain and return the potatoes to the saucepan. Cook over low heat for 1–2 minutes to remove any remaining moisture. Mash well.

- In a mixing bowl, combine the mashed potato, fish, spring onions, parsley, lemon zest and juice, mustard and egg yolk. Season well with salt and freshly ground black pepper.

- Press the mixture firmly into eight patties. Lightly coat each patty in the flour and shake off any excess.

- Whisk together the beaten egg and milk in a shallow bowl. Place the breadcrumbs in a second shallow bowl.

- Dip each fishcake into the egg mixture and then into the breadcrumbs, making sure each is well coated. Refrigerate for 20 minutes, or until ready to cook.

- Heat the oil in a frying pan over medium heat. Cook the fish cakes, in batches if necessary, for 3–4 minutes on each side, or until golden. Serve with lemon wedges, a little homemade mayonnaise (see page 106) and a green salad.

- Fish cakes are also delicious made with either tinned or freshly cooked salmon.

SERVES 4

fish pie.

4 cups mashed potato (see page 136)

1 pound firm white fish fillets

½ pound smoked fish (haddock or cod) fillets

2½ cups milk

1 bay leaf

4 black peppercorns

4 tablespoons butter

1 small onion, chopped

¼ cup plain (all-purpose) flour

½ pound small cooked shrimp, shelled

pinch of cayenne pepper

2 tablespoons chopped flat-leaf parsley

salt and freshly ground black pepper

3 hard-boiled eggs, peeled and quartered

2 tablespoons butter, extra

- First, make the mashed potato according to the instructions on page 136.

- Preheat the oven to 350°F.

- Place the white fish, smoked fish, milk, bay leaf, and peppercorns in a saucepan over medium heat. Bring to a boil then reduce the heat and simmer for 5 minutes. Strain the mixture, reserving the fish and the strained milk.

- Skin the fish, remove any bones, flake into bite-sized pieces and place in a bowl.

- Melt the butter in a clean saucepan over low–medium heat. Add the onion and cook for 7 minutes, stirring frequently, until soft and translucent. Add the flour, stir well, and cook for 1 minute. Slowly whisk in the reserved milk. Bring the mixture to a boil, whisking frequently, until smooth and thick. Allow to cool.

- Add the shrimp, cayenne pepper, and parsley to the bowl containing the fish, and pour over the white sauce. Season well with salt and freshly ground black pepper.

- Spoon the mixture into a large soufflé dish or other ovenproof dish. Top with the boiled egg pieces. Spread with the mashed potato and fluff up with a fork. Dot with the extra butter. Bake for 30–35 minutes, or until golden and bubbling.

SERVES 4-6

french toast.

These slices of thick bread, dipped in a rich mix of egg, milk, sugar, and vanilla, make a delicious, indulgent start to the day—especially when delivered to your bed on a tray.

4 eggs	salt
2 tablespoons sugar	4 slices white or multigrain bread
½ cup milk or cream	unsalted butter, for frying
½ teaspoon vanilla extract	maple syrup, to serve

- In a shallow bowl, mix together the eggs, sugar, milk, vanilla, and a pinch of salt.

- Heat a little butter in a frying pan over medium heat. Dip two slices of bread in the egg mixture for 30–60 seconds, or until the mixture is well absorbed by the bread. Fry the soaked bread for 1 minute on each side, or until crisp and golden. Repeat with the remaining slices of bread.

- Serve warm, drizzled with maple syrup.

French toast is delicious served with a little crispy bacon or fresh berries on the side.

—

Slices of brioche or split croissants instead of the bread make a good variation.

SERVES 2

french vinaigrette.

A French dressing or vinaigrette is simply a combination of oil and vinegar, held together with a little Dijon mustard and seasoned with salt and pepper. The classic proportion for a French dressing is one part vinegar (or an acidic juice such as lemon juice) to three parts oil.

2 tablespoons vinegar or lemon juice	½ cup olive oil
1 teaspoon Dijon mustard	

- Place the vinegar or lemon juice, mustard, and olive oil in a screw-top jar. Season with salt and freshly ground black pepper. Put the lid on the jar and shake well to combine. The vinaigrette will keep for 4–5 days in the fridge.

Vary the types of oil and vinegar you use. When choosing the oil and vinegar, remember they should complement each other. The rich texture and fruity taste of extra-virgin olive oil is well balanced by balsamic vinegar, whereas nut oils are good combined with fruit vinegars. Chili- or herb-flavored oils are balanced by the use of wine vinegars or lemon juice.

—

The oil and vinegar will separate on standing, so store in a screw-top jar and shake well just before adding to a salad.

—

Use crushed garlic, chopped fresh chilies, or chopped fresh herbs to add variety to the dressing.

SERVES 4

frittata.

Frittatas can vary from thin and pancake-like to thick with a golden crust and creamy center. The following recipe for this popular Italian omelette is a classic flavor combination and is perfect picnic fare.

6 large eggs	pinch of freshly grated nutmeg
2½ cups baby spinach leaves, roughly chopped	salt and freshly ground black pepper
1¼ cups freshly grated parmesan	1 tablespoon olive oil

- In a mixing bowl, beat the eggs lightly with a fork. Add the spinach, 1 cup of the parmesan and the nutmeg. Season to taste with salt and freshly ground black pepper.

- Heat the olive oil in a 9" nonstick frying pan over medium heat. Swirl the pan to coat with oil. Pour in the egg mixture. Reduce the heat to low and cook, stirring once, for 12–15 minutes. The bottom should be firm and the top a little runny. Sprinkle with the remaining ¼ cup of parmesan.

- Place the frying pan under a preheated broiler for just long enough to set the top. A good frittata should be firm but moist, never stiff and dry. Remove from the heat and allow to cool for 2 minutes. Serve straight from the pan, or place a large, flat plate over the top of the pan and invert the frittata onto it. Serve warm or at room temperature, sliced into wedges.

Variations on this recipe are only limited by what ingredients you have at hand. Try incorporating cooked zucchini, sautéed mushrooms, cooked asparagus, prosciutto, marinated artichokes, goat's cheese, or cooked potato slices.

SERVES 4

fruit cake.

1 cup unsalted butter, chopped

1 cup lightly packed brown sugar

½ cup brandy

2 pounds mixed dried fruit

3½ ounces mixed peel

3½ ounces maraschino cherries, halved

5 eggs, beaten

2 tablespoons light molasses

2 teaspoons finely grated lemon zest

2 tablespoons finely grated orange zest

2¼ cups plain (all-purpose) flour

¾ teaspoon baking powder

1 teaspoon baking soda

⅛ teaspoon salt

1½ teaspoons mixed spice

1 cup almonds

- Place the butter, sugar, brandy, dried fruit, mixed peel, cherries, and ½ cup of water in a large saucepan. Bring to a boil and simmer gently, stirring frequently, for 10 minutes. Allow to cool.

- Preheat the oven to 300°F. Grease a 9" round cake pan. Line the base and sides with a double layer of baking paper, extending the paper 2" above the cake pan.

- Transfer the cool fruit mixture to a large mixing bowl. Add the beaten eggs, molasses, lemon and orange zest, and mix well. Sift the flour, baking powder, baking soda, salt, and mixed spice into the bowl and mix until combined. Roughly chop half the almonds and stir these into the mixture. Spoon the mixture into the prepared cake pan. Decorate the top of the cake with the remaining whole almonds. Wrap the cake pan in a double layer of brown paper, extending the paper 2" above the cake pan, to match the baking paper. Tie securely with string.

- Bake for 2–2½ hours, or until firm and a wooden skewer inserted into the center comes out clean. Allow to cool in the pan. Wrap in foil and store for up to 3 months in a cool, dark place.

A good combination of mixed dried fruit is 12 ounces of chopped raisins, 8 ounces of unsulphured apricots, 8 ounces of currants, and 4 ounces of chopped dates, figs, and prunes.

SERVES 12-16

fruit tart.

1 sheet frozen puff pastry, thawed	2 tablespoons sugar
2 tablespoons apricot jam	2 tablespoons unsalted butter
3 ripe nectarines or plums	

- Preheat the oven to 400°F. Place the puffed pastry onto a lightly greased baking sheet.

- Place the jam and 2 tablespoons of water in a small saucepan and warm until the mixture forms a syrup. Brush half the syrup over the sheet of pastry, leaving a ¾" border all around.

- Halve the nectarines or plums, remove the seeds and thinly slice the fruit. Lay the slices, overlapping slightly, over the pastry, again leaving a ¾" border all around. Sprinkle over the sugar and dot the fruit with the butter.

- Bake the tart for 20–25 minutes, or until the pastry is golden and puffed up. Glaze the tart by brushing lightly with the remaining jam. Cut into slices and serve warm or at room temperature with cream or ice cream.

Two peeled and thinly sliced pears or apples may be substituted for the stone fruit.

SERVES 4

garlic bread.

1 medium French baguette

salt and freshly ground black pepper

GARLIC BUTTER

³/₄ cup unsalted butter, softened

4 cloves garlic, chopped

2 tablespoons finely chopped
flat-leaf parsley

1 teaspoon lemon juice

- Preheat the oven to 350°F.

- To make the garlic butter, mix together the ingredients thoroughly in a small mixing bowl. Season with salt and freshly ground black pepper.

- Cut slashes into the baguette at 1" intervals, cutting almost to the bottom crust, and spread each side of the cut liberally with the garlic butter.

- Wrap the bread in foil and bake for 10 minutes. Open the foil at the top and bake for another 5–7 minutes, or until crisp. Serve immediately.

Any leftover garlic butter can be rolled in foil and kept in the fridge for up to 2 weeks.

—

Add a little finely chopped chili or a dash of Tabasco sauce to the garlic butter for a hotter version.

SERVES 4

garlic shrimp.

The combination of butter, garlic, and parsley is a true classic.

24 large uncooked shrimp

6 tablespoons unsalted butter

2 tablespoons olive oil

3 cloves garlic, finely chopped

½ large red chili, seeded and finely chopped

2 tablespoons chopped flat-leaf parsley

juice of 1 lemon

sea salt and freshly ground black pepper

1 tablespoon chopped flat-leaf parsley, extra

2 teaspoons finely grated lemon zest

- Peel and devein the shrimp, leaving the tails intact. Set aside.

- Melt the butter and olive oil in a large frying pan or wok over medium heat. Add the garlic and chili and cook, stirring, for 3 minutes. Add the shrimp and cook, untouched, for 2 minutes. Turn the shrimp, add the parsley, and squeeze over the lemon juice. Cook for 2–3 minutes longer, or until the shrimp is pink. Season with sea salt and freshly ground black pepper.

- In a small bowl, combine the extra chopped parsley and the lemon zest, and sprinkle this mixture over the shrimp. Serve at once with good crusty bread to mop up the juices.

As a variation, add ½ teaspoon of grated fresh ginger at the beginning with the garlic and chili. Cook as above, but replace the lemon with lime, and the parsley with cilantro.

—

Fresh scallops are also delicious cooked this way.

SERVES 4

gazpacho.

Few dishes taste as refreshing on a hot summer's day as this simple, no-cook, chilled soup.

2 pounds ripe tomatoes, peeled and chopped

1 small cucumber, roughly chopped

1 red bell pepper, seeded and chopped

2 cloves garlic, chopped

½ red onion, chopped

2 thick slices good white bread

¼ cup sherry vinegar or red wine vinegar

salt and freshly ground black pepper

extra-virgin olive oil, to drizzle

- Place the tomatoes, cucumber, pepper, garlic, and onion in a large mixing bowl. Remove the crusts from the bread. Chop the bread and add it to the bowl. Stir in 1½ cups of water.

- Transfer the mixture to a food processor or blender and pulse until the mixture is roughly combined. (This may need to be done in batches.) The mixture should still be slightly chunky. Add a little extra water if the soup needs thinning.

- Chill for at least 2 hours, or preferably overnight, to allow the flavors to develop.

- Just before serving, stir in the vinegar. Season to taste with salt and freshly ground black pepper. Serve well chilled with a good drizzle of extra-virgin olive oil.

To peel tomatoes, use a sharp knife to cut a cross in the base of each tomato. Place in a heatproof bowl and cover with boiling water. Leave for 45 seconds, then transfer to cold water and peel the skin away, beginning at the cross.

—

Decent tomatoes are essential for a good gazpacho. If possible, use homegrown ones.

—

Crabmeat or cooked shrimp is a delicious addition to this soup.

SERVES 4

ginger cake.

This cake is a great addition to your recipe collection. It's delicious and easy to make—it falls into that stress-free "melt and mix" category of baking.

¼ cup unsalted butter, cubed	½ teaspoon mixed spice
½ cup honey or golden syrup	½ cup sugar
1 cup plain (all-purpose) flour	⅛ teaspoon salt
½ teaspoon baking powder	½ cup milk
1 teaspoon baking soda	1 egg, beaten
1 heaped teaspoon ground ginger	

- Preheat the oven to 325°F. Thoroughly grease a 9" x 5" loaf pan and line the base with baking paper.

- Place the butter and honey in a small saucepan. Melt, stirring occasionally, over low heat. Remove from the heat.

- Sift the flour, the baking powder, baking soda, and the spices into a mixing bowl. Add the sugar and salt, then add the milk and egg and mix until smooth. Gradually add the melted butter mixture, stirring until well incorporated.

- Pour the batter into the prepared loaf pan and bake for 50–55 minutes, or until risen and firm to the touch. A wooden skewer inserted into the middle of the cake should come out clean. Allow the cake to cool in the pan for 5 minutes before turning out onto a wire rack to cool. Serve dusted with confectioners' sugar.

If you like, you can turn this into a simple syrup cake. Place ½ cup of sugar, ½ cup of water, and 1 tablespoon of finely grated fresh ginger in a small saucepan. Bring the mixture to a boil and simmer for 5 minutes. Spoon a little syrup over the hot cake.

SERVES 8

gingerbread cookies.

½ cup unsalted butter

¼ cup honey or golden syrup

⅓ lightly packed brown sugar

2¼ cups plain (all-purpose) flour

½ teaspoon baking powder

1 tablespoon baking soda

1 tablespoon ground ginger

½ teaspoon mixed spice

⅛ teaspoon salt

1 egg, lightly beaten

■ Place the butter, honey, and brown sugar in a small saucepan over low heat. Cook, stirring, until the butter has melted and the mixture is smooth. Remove from the heat and allow to cool.

■ Sift the flour, the baking powder, baking soda, the spices, and the salt into a large mixing bowl and make a well in the center. Pour in the melted butter mixture and the beaten egg and mix well.

■ Turn out onto a lightly floured surface and knead until smooth. Wrap in plastic wrap and refrigerate for 30 minutes.

■ Preheat the oven to 325°F. Line two oven trays with baking paper.

■ Roll out the dough between two sheets of baking paper to a thickness of ¼". Cut out shapes with cookie cutters and bake for 8–10 minutes, or until firm and golden brown. Allow to cool on a wire rack.

To decorate your cookies, beat 1 egg white with an electric mixer until foamy. Gradually add 1 teaspoon of lemon juice and 1½ cups of sifted confectioners' sugar, beating all the while until the mixture is thick and smooth. Tint the mixture with a couple of drops of food coloring. Attach a fine nozzle to a piping bag and pipe decorative shapes onto the cookies.

MAKES 24-30

granola.

The perfect granola should be chewy, crisp, and crumbly, with a combination of sweet and tart flavors. The trick is selecting the right ingredients and combining them in the proper proportions. Try this basic recipe, substituting different nuts, seeds, or fruit as desired.

3 cups rolled oats	$\frac{1}{4}$ cup wheat germ
1 cup almonds	1 teaspoon finely grated lemon zest
$\frac{1}{2}$ cup roughly chopped pecans	$\frac{1}{3}$ cup vegetable oil
$\frac{1}{2}$ cup shredded coconut	$\frac{1}{2}$ cup honey
2 tablespoons sesame seeds	1 cup chopped dried apricots
2 tablespoons pepitas (pumpkin seeds)	1 cup raisins

- Preheat the oven to 325°F.

- Place the oats, almonds, pecans, coconut, sesame seeds, pepitas, wheat germ, and lemon zest in a large mixing bowl.

- In a small saucepan over low heat, warm the vegetable oil and honey.

- Pour the honey mixture over the oat mixture and mix thoroughly.

- Tip the mixture onto a baking sheet and bake, stirring every 5 minutes, for 20 minutes, or until golden. Allow the mixture to cool completely.

- Mix in the apricots and raisins.

- Granola can be stored in an airtight container for up to 3 months.

When experimenting with different combinations of ingredients, keep in mind that the total volume of nuts and fruit should be equal to or slightly greater than the volume of oats.

—

Vary the dried fruit component by using dried apples, pears, peaches, or cranberries.

MAKES 8 CUPS

gravy.

pan juices from roast meat

2-3 tablespoons plain (all-purpose) flour

½ cup wine

2 cups stock or water

salt and freshly ground black pepper

- After removing the roasted meat from the roasting pan, pour off all but about ½ cup of the fat. Place the roasting pan over medium heat on the stove top and sprinkle over the flour. Stir constantly with a wooden spoon for 1–2 minutes, or until the flour has browned slightly.

- Gradually add the wine and stock, stirring constantly to loosen any browned bits stuck to the bottom of the pan, until the gravy has thickened and is smooth. Simmer gently for 5–10 minutes, adding a little extra stock or water if necessary to reach the desired consistency. Season to taste with salt and freshly ground black pepper.

As a rule, use white wine to make gravy for poultry dishes and red wine for red meat dishes.

SERVES 4-6

guacamole.

2 ripe avocados

juice of 2 limes

1 large green chili, seeded
and finely chopped

¼ cup finely chopped flat-leaf parsley
or cilantro

3 scallions, finely chopped

1 tablespoon olive oil

salt and freshly ground black pepper

- Cut avocados lengthwise in half; remove the pit and peel. Chop the flesh and transfer to a small bowl. Add the lime juice, chili, parsley or cilantro, and scallions. Mash together with a fork, gradually incorporating the olive oil.

- Season to taste with salt and freshly ground black pepper, and add a little extra lime juice if needed.

Add 2–3 drops of Tabasco sauce if you like a hotter guacamole.

MAKES 1 CUP

hollandaise sauce.

Hollandaise sauce is wonderful served with fish, steamed asparagus, or with poached eggs, as in eggs Benedict.

| ½ cup unsalted butter | 3 egg yolks |
| 1 tablespoon lemon juice | salt and freshly ground black pepper |

- Melt the butter in a small saucepan over low heat. Pour the melted butter into a small cup, leaving behind any white sediment in the bottom of the pan. Allow to cool slightly.

- Place the lemon juice, egg yolks, and 1 tablespoon of water in a heatproof bowl over a saucepan of simmering water. Whisk the yolk mixture until combined. Gradually add the melted butter, whisking until the sauce is smooth and thick. If the sauce thickens too much, whisk in a spoonful of hot water. Do not allow the mixture to boil or the sauce will separate. Season to taste with salt and freshly ground black pepper, and keep warm until ready to serve.

You can make hollandaise sauce in a food processor or blender by processing the lemon juice, egg yolks, and 1 tablespoon of water in the machine. While the machine is running, gradually add the warm melted butter until the sauce is smooth and thick. Season to taste with salt and freshly ground black pepper.

—

To make orange hollandaise, replace the lemon juice with 2 tablespoons of strained freshly squeezed orange juice and proceed as above.

MAKES 1 CUP

hummus.

1 14-ounce can chickpeas (garbanzo beans), drained and rinsed

3 cloves garlic, crushed

¼ cup lemon juice

¼ cup tahini (sesame paste)

1 teaspoon ground cumin

pinch cayenne pepper

¼ cup olive oil

salt and freshly ground black pepper

- Place the chickpeas, garlic, lemon juice, tahini, cumin, and cayenne pepper in the bowl of a food processor. With the motor running, slowly add the olive oil and process until smooth. Add a little extra oil or lemon juice if the mixture is too thick. Season to taste with salt and freshly ground black pepper.

- Serve with pita bread. Leftover hummus can be stored in an airtight container in the refrigerator for 2–3 days.

MAKES 1 CUP

lamb, roasted leg.

3 cloves garlic, peeled	2 tablespoons olive oil
1 medium-sized bone-in leg of lamb (3 pounds)	salt and freshly ground black pepper
6–8 sprigs rosemary	assorted vegetables, peeled and chopped, to roast

- Preheat the oven to 400°F.

- Cut each garlic clove into three slivers. With the point of a small sharp knife, make six to eight incisions in the lamb. Insert the garlic slivers and a small sprig of rosemary into each of the cuts.

- Rub the skin of the lamb with 1 tablespoon of the oil. Season with salt and freshly ground black pepper.

- Place the lamb in a large roasting pan and surround with a selection of peeled and chopped vegetables. Drizzle the vegetables with the remaining oil. Roast the lamb for 65–75 minutes, basting occasionally with the pan juices.

- Remove the lamb from the pan, cover with foil and allow to rest for 10 minutes before carving. Keep the vegetables warm until ready to serve.

- To make gravy, refer to the instructions on page 91.

- Slice the lamb into medium–thick slices, serve with vegetables and accompany with gravy and mint sauce, if desired. If you have someone who is an expert carver, a roast leg of lamb looks magnificent presented at the table on a large platter surrounded by vegetables.

Carrots, potatoes, Jerusalem artichokes, parsnips, rutabagas, pearl onions, and chunks of sweet potato are all delicious roasted along with the lamb.

SERVES 4-6

lasagna.

4 tablespoons unsalted butter

⅓ cup plain (all-purpose) flour

2½ cups milk

pinch of freshly grated nutmeg

salt and freshly ground black pepper

1 pound lasagna noodles

6 cups bolognese sauce (see page 19)

¾ cup freshly grated parmesan

- Melt the butter in a medium-sized saucepan and stir in the flour. Cook over medium heat, stirring constantly, for 1 minute. Remove from the heat and gradually add the milk, stirring constantly. Return to the heat and bring to a boil, stirring frequently. Simmer for 2 minutes, or until the sauce has thickened. Add the nutmeg and season well with salt and freshly ground black pepper. Set aside.

- Cook the noodles, two at a time, in a large saucepan of boiling salted water for 2 minutes. Remove and refresh by placing in a large bowl of iced water for 2 minutes. Dry well with kitchen paper.

- Preheat the oven to 350°F. Lightly grease a 12" x 8½" x 2" baking dish.

- Place a layer of the noodles over the base of the dish. Cover with a thin layer of bolognese sauce and top with another layer of noodles. Continue to layer the lasagna and the sauce–there should be enough for five layers of each. Top with the white sauce and sprinkle with the parmesan. Bake for 35–40 minutes, or until golden and bubbling. Allow to stand for 10 minutes before serving.

You can make and cook lasagna ahead of time and reheat in a 350°F oven for 15–20 minutes.

SERVES 6

lemon cake.

1½ cups plain (all-purpose) flour, sifted

2¼ teaspoons baking powder

¼ teaspoon salt

¾ cup unsalted butter, softened

¾ cup sugar

1 tablespoon finely grated lemon zest

3 eggs, lightly beaten

½ cup sugar

¼ cup lemon juice

- Preheat the oven to 325°F. Grease a 9" x 5" loaf pan and line the base with baking paper.

- In a medium bowl, combine the flour, baking powder, and salt.

- In a large bowl with an electric mixer, beat the butter, sugar, and lemon zest for 2–3 minutes, or until soft and well mixed. Gradually add the beaten eggs, alternating with a spoonful of the flour mixture, mixing well after each addition. Fold in the remaining flour and mix gently until smooth.

- Spoon the batter into the prepared loaf pan and smooth the surface. Bake for 50–60 minutes, or until golden and firm to the touch. A wooden skewer inserted in the center should come out clean. Turn out onto a wire rack.

- Mix together the sugar and lemon juice until just combined, without letting the sugar dissolve. Quickly spoon the sugar mixture over the top of the warm cake. The juice will sink into the cake and the sugar will form a crunchy topping.

SERVES 8

lemon curd.

Lemon curd makes a great filling for cakes or small tarts or a topping for ice cream or pavlova. Alternatively, simply spread onto buttered bread, hot toast, scones, or English muffins.

3 lemons	½ cup unsalted butter
1 cup sugar	3 eggs, lightly beaten

■ Wash and dry the lemons. Finely grate the zest of one of the lemons. Place the zest, along with the sugar and butter, in a small, heavy-based saucepan over very low heat. Stir with a wooden spoon until the butter has melted and the sugar has dissolved.

■ Squeeze the three lemons and strain the juice. Add the juice and beaten eggs to the saucepan. Continue to cook over low heat, stirring constantly, until the mixture is thick enough to coat the back of the spoon. Do not allow the mixture to boil.

■ Stir the mixture well, pour into clean screw-top jars, and seal. Allow to cool to room temperature before storing in the refrigerator for up to 1 month.

Lemon curd requires slow cooking and constant stirring, so don't rush the process by increasing the heat.

—

To make lime curd, substitute the lemon zest with the zest of 2 limes, and the lemon juice with the juice of 5 medium-sized limes.

—

To make orange curd, substitute the lemon zest with 1 tablespoon of finely grated orange zest, and the lemon juice with the juice of 2 medium-sized oranges.

—

To make passionfruit curd, substitute the lemon juice with the strained pulp of 8 passionfruit and the unstrained pulp of 2 passionfruit.

MAKES 1½ CUPS

lemon delicious pudding.

This simple dessert consists of a rich, creamy lemon base topped
with a light golden sponge.

¼ cup plain (all-purpose) flour	3 eggs, separated
½ teaspoon baking powder	2 teaspoons finely grated lemon zest
⅛ teaspoon salt	¾ cup milk
4 tablespoons unsalted butter, softened	⅓ cup lemon juice
¾ cup sugar	

- Preheat the oven to 350°F. Grease a deep 5-cup-capacity soufflé dish.

- In a small mixing bowl, combine the flour, baking powder, and salt.

- In a large bowl with an electric mixer, beat the butter, sugar, egg yolks, and lemon zest until light and fluffy. Fold in the flour mixture alternating with the milk to make a smooth batter. Stir in the lemon juice. The batter may look like it has separated at this stage, but this is fine.

- In a separate clean bowl, whisk the egg whites until firm. Gently fold the whites into the batter.

- Pour the batter into the prepared dish. Place the dish in a large baking pan and fill the pan with enough boiling water to come a third of the way up the sides of the dish. Carefully transfer to the oven and bake for 50–55 minutes, or until the top is golden and risen. Dust with confectioners' sugar and serve with cream.

*This pudding may also be cooked in six individual dishes, which take about
30 minutes to cook.*

—

Lime zest and juice can be substituted for the lemon, if you prefer.

SERVES 6

lemon tart.

1 sweet shortcrust pastry (see page 119)	2 tablespoons finely grated lemon zest
4 eggs	1¼ cups lemon juice
2 egg yolks	½ cup cream
1 cup sugar	

- Prepare the pastry according to the instructions on page 119. Chill the pastry for at least 30 minutes before using.

- Lightly grease a 10" loose-based tart pan. Roll out the pastry between two sheets of baking paper so that it is large enough to fit the tart pan. Line the pan with the pastry, leaving a little pastry overhanging the pan. Refrigerate for 15 minutes.

- Preheat the oven to 400°F.

- Line the pastry shell with baking paper. Half-fill the pastry shell with pie weights, uncooked dried beans or rice, and bake for 12 minutes. Remove the weights and baking paper, return the pan to the oven and cook for 10–15 minutes longer, or until the pastry is dry and lightly colored. Set aside to cool. If the pastry shell has any holes, plug them with a little uncooked pastry. With a sharp knife, cut off the overhanging pastry.

- Reduce the oven temperature to 300°F.

- Whisk together the whole eggs, egg yolks, and sugar until well combined. Whisk in the lemon zest and juice. Stir in the cream. Place the tart pan on a flat oven tray. Pour the egg and lemon mixture into the pastry shell, filling almost to the top of the tart shell. Bake for 35–40 minutes, or until it is just set—the center should wobble a little. The tart will firm up as it cools. Allow to cool for at least 1 hour before serving. Serve dusted with confectioners' sugar.

SERVES 8

lemonade.

Pop six extra lemons into your basket next time you go shopping. Homemade lemonade is worth making, not only for its simplicity but because of its ability to refresh and revive. The following recipe gives you a concentrated base. Pour a little into a glass or jug, add ice and top off with spring or sparkling water to taste.

1½ cups sugar │ 6 lemons

- Place the sugar and 1½ cups of water in a small saucepan. Finely grate the zest of two of the lemons and add this to the saucepan. Bring the mixture to a boil, stirring constantly. Simmer for 5 minutes, or until the sugar has dissolved.

- Squeeze the juice of all six lemons and add to the saucepan. Allow to cool.

- Strain the mixture into a bottle, seal, and store in the refrigerator for up to 5 days. Dilute as required.

Choose ripe, bright yellow lemons that feel heavy for their size.

—

Add some freshly chopped mint leaves as a tasty variation.

—

Try this syrup with a dash of gin or vodka and diluted with soda or tonic water.

MAKES 3 CUPS CONCENTRATED SYRUP

mayonnaise.

Mayonnaise is simple to make at home. I mix it by hand with a wire whisk, rather than whizzing it in the food processor, because I prefer the silky texture of a handmade mayonnaise.

2 egg yolks	¼ cup olive oil
1 teaspoon Dijon mustard	¾ cup vegetable oil
1 tablespoon lemon juice	freshly ground black pepper
salt	

- Place the egg yolks, mustard, lemon juice, and a pinch of salt into a small bowl and whisk until smooth.

- Combine the olive oil and vegetable oil in a jar. Pour it very slowly, drop by drop, into the egg mixture, whisking constantly. As the mixture thickens, start adding the oil in a steady stream. Continue until all the oil has been incorporated and the mixture is thick. Season to taste with salt and freshly ground black pepper. Taste and add a little more lemon juice if desired. The mixture can be thinned with boiling water, if necessary.

It's a good idea to stand the mixing bowl on a damp cloth while you're making mayonnaise. This prevents it from moving as you whisk.

—

The mixture may separate if the oil has been added too quickly. To remedy this, simply whisk up another egg yolk and gradually whisk this through the separated mixture in small amounts.

—

Mayonnaise can easily be flavored. Chopped fresh herbs, garlic, anchovies, lemon zest, capers, or chili are just a few suggestions.

MAKES 1½ CUPS

meatballs.

1 thick slice Italian-style bread	1 large egg, lightly beaten
milk, to soak	salt and freshly ground black pepper
1¼ pounds ground veal	plain (all-purpose) flour, to coat
2 cloves garlic, finely chopped	2–3 tablespoons olive oil
⅓ cup freshly grated parmesan	1 13-ounce can crushed tomatoes
2 tablespoons chopped flat-leaf parsley	2 cloves garlic, peeled, extra
	6½ ounces mozzarella, sliced or grated
1 tablespoon chopped oregano	chopped flat-leaf parsley, extra, to garnish
1 teaspoon finely grated lemon zest	

- Remove the crust from the bread, break the bread into pieces, and soak in a little milk. Squeeze dry, crumble, and place in a large bowl. Add the ground veal, garlic, parmesan, parsley, oregano, lemon zest, and beaten egg, and mix well. Season with plenty of salt and freshly ground black pepper. To check the seasoning, fry a small amount of the mixture until cooked thoroughly and the beef is no longer pink in the center. Taste it; adjust the seasoning as desired.

- Shape the mixture into balls 2" in diameter. Roll them in flour and shake off any excess.

- Heat the oil in a large frying pan over medium heat. Add the meatballs and cook, turning, until brown all over. Remove and drain on kitchen paper.

- Add the crushed tomatoes and whole garlic cloves to the frying pan. Bring to a boil, reduce the heat, and simmer gently for 5 minutes. Return the meatballs to the pan and cook, turning them occasionally, for 5 minutes.

- Preheat the oven to 350°F.

- Transfer the meatballs and sauce to an ovenproof dish. Top with the mozzarella and bake for 20 minutes. Sprinkle with the extra chopped parsley and serve with crusty bread to mop up the juices.

SERVES 4-6

minestrone.

2 tablespoons olive oil

3 slices bacon or pancetta, chopped

2 small onions, chopped

1 leek, sliced

1 carrot, chopped

2 ribs celery, chopped

1 clove garlic, crushed

2 zucchini, diced

1 13-ounce can crushed tomatoes

6 cups chicken stock
(see page 39)

2 cups shredded spinach leaves

4 ounces small pasta shapes,
such as orzo

1 13-ounce can cannellini beans, rinsed
and drained

2 tablespoons chopped flat-leaf
parsley or basil

salt and freshly ground black pepper

extra-virgin olive oil, to serve

freshly grated parmesan, to serve

- Heat the oil in a large saucepan over low heat. Add the bacon or pancetta and cook, stirring, for 2 minutes. Add the onion, leek, carrot, celery, and garlic. Cook, stirring, for 7–8 minutes, or until softened. This mixture gives the soup its flavor base.

- Add the zucchini and crushed tomatoes to the saucepan. Cook, stirring, for 2 minutes. Add the chicken stock and 2 cups of water. Bring to a boil. Skim off any foam, reduce the heat, and simmer gently for 30 minutes.

- Add the spinach and pasta. Simmer for 20 minutes, stirring occasionally.

- Add the cannellini beans and parsley. Add extra water or stock if there is not enough liquid, but remember, this is a thick soup. Season to taste with salt and freshly ground black pepper. Continue to cook for 10 minutes longer.

- Ladle the soup into bowls, drizzle with extra-virgin olive oil, and sprinkle with freshly grated parmesan.

SERVES 4–6

muffins.

Muffins are fast, easy, and infinitely variable.

2¼ cups plain (all-purpose) flour	2 eggs
2 teaspoons baking powder	1 teaspoon vanilla extract
½ teaspoon baking soda	¾ cup lightly packed brown sugar
salt	½ cup unsalted butter, melted
1¼ cups buttermilk	

- Preheat the oven to 375°F. Grease a 12-cup muffin pan or line with paper baking cups.

- Sift the flour, baking powder, baking soda, and a pinch of salt into a mixing bowl and make a well in the center.

- Whisk together the buttermilk, eggs, vanilla, sugar, and melted butter. Pour the egg mixture into the well in the flour mixture and stir until the ingredients are just combined. Do not over-mix—the batter should not be smooth.

- Divide the mixture evenly between the muffin cups. Bake for 20–25 minutes, or until the tops are golden and a wooden skewer inserted into the center of a muffin comes out clean. Allow to cool in the pan for 5 minutes before turning out onto a wire rack. Muffins are delicious served warm.

If you can't find buttermilk, use ½ cup of plain yogurt mixed with ¾ cup of milk.

—

To make blueberry muffins, fold ½ cup of fresh or frozen blueberries into the batter.

—

To make pecan muffins, fold in ¾ cup of chopped pecans. Sprinkle the top of each muffin with a little ground cinnamon and extra chopped nuts before baking.

MAKES 12

mussels.

Mussels are perfect for a simple, fast, and easy supper. For two people you will need 2–2½ pounds of fresh mussels. Choose mussels that have perfect shells and that close firmly after they've been given a good tap. Soak the mussels in fresh water for 15 minutes, and then pull off their beards with a sharp tug.

2 tablespoons olive oil	2½ pounds fresh mussels, cleaned and debearded
1 onion, chopped	
2 cloves garlic, crushed	salt and freshly ground black pepper
1 tablespoon chopped flat-leaf parsley	chopped flat-leaf parsley, extra, to serve
1 cup white wine	
¼ cup cream	

- Place a large saucepan or wok over medium heat. Add the oil, onion, garlic, parsley, wine, and cream. Bring to a boil and simmer for 5 minutes. Add the mussels and increase the heat to high. Cover with a tight-fitting lid and cook for 3 minutes, giving the pan an occasional shake to help the mussels release their flavor.

- Uncover and stir well. As the mussels open, transfer them to two deep serving bowls. Discard any that haven't opened after 5 minutes. Boil the broth for 2 minutes, season to taste with salt and freshly ground black pepper, and then strain over the mussels. Discard the solids. Sprinkle the mussels with the extra chopped parsley and serve immediately. Serve with crusty bread to mop up the delicious creamy broth.

Live, fresh mussels are generally available year-round on the East Coast. On the West Coast, the mussel season is November through April.

SERVES 2

oatmeal coconut cookies.

These delicious oat and coconut cookies are perfect served with a tall glass of milk or your favorite cup of tea.

1 cup plain (all-purpose) flour	1/4 cup honey or golden syrup
1 cup rolled oats	1/2 cup unsalted butter, cubed
1 cup shredded coconut	1 teaspoon baking soda
3/4 cup sugar	2 tablespoons boiling water
salt	

- Preheat the oven to 350°F. Line two baking trays with baking paper.

- Sift the flour into a mixing bowl and stir in the oats, coconut, sugar, and a pinch of salt. Make a well in the center.

- Place the honey and butter in a small saucepan. Stir over low heat until the butter has melted. In a cup, dissolve the baking soda in the boiling water and add to the butter mixture. The mixture will foam a little.

- Pour the butter mixture into the well in the center of the dry ingredients and stir with a wooden spoon until combined. Add a little extra water if the mixture is dry.

- Drop tablespoonfuls of the mixture onto the prepared trays, leaving 1 1/4" between each to allow for spreading.

- Bake for 12–15 minutes, or until golden. Allow to cool on the trays for a few minutes before transferring to wire racks to cool completely. Store in an airtight container for up to 2 weeks.

MAKES 30

olives, marinated.

1 pound black or green olives

3 cloves garlic, finely sliced

1 large red chili, seeded and finely chopped

2 teaspoons finely grated lemon zest

2 teaspoons chopped rosemary

3 sprigs thyme

2 bay leaves

olive oil, to cover

■ In a mixing bowl, combine the olives, garlic, chili, lemon zest, rosemary, thyme, and bay leaves, then spoon into a large glass jar. Add enough olive oil to cover the olives. Seal the jar and tap gently to dislodge any air bubbles.

Marinate in the refrigerator for 1–2 weeks before eating.

You can use many other flavor combinations for this versatile dish. Grated orange zest, basil leaves, or anchovies are just a few other ingredients that work well. Vary the recipe above with one or more of these ingredients.

pancakes.

1 cup plain (all-purpose) flour	2 eggs, lightly beaten
1 teaspoon baking powder	1 cup milk
salt	2 tablespoons butter, melted
2 tablespoons sugar (optional)	

- Sift the flour, baking powder, and a pinch of salt into a bowl. Stir in the sugar if you wish to make sweet pancakes. Make a well in the center.

- In a separate bowl, combine the beaten eggs, milk, and melted butter. Pour the wet ingredients into the dry ingredients and mix until a smooth batter forms.

- Grease a small nonstick frying pan and preheat over moderate heat for 1 minute.

- Ladle the batter into the pan and cook for about 1 minute, or until bubbles appear on the pancake and the underside is golden. Using a spatula, flip the pancake and cook for 45–60 seconds longer before serving.

The pancake batter can be made ahead of time and left to rest for up to 2 hours.
Serve sweet pancakes with maple syrup, or try a squeeze of lemon juice and
a sprinkling of sugar.

—

For savory pancakes, fill with ratatouille or mushrooms cooked in a little cream.
A little grated zucchini, chopped fresh herbs, or scallions
added to the batter also make delicious variations.

MAKES 6-8

pastry, shortcrust.

Shortcrust pastry is easy to make and is suitable for tarts, pies, or quiches. Sweet shortcrust is enriched with a little sugar and a beaten egg, which makes it perfect for sweet tarts (see recipe variation below).

2 cups plain (all-purpose) flour	½ cup butter, chilled and diced
salt	3-4 tablespoons chilled water

■ Sift the flour and a pinch of salt into a large bowl. Rub the butter into the flour mixture with your fingertips until it resembles fine breadcrumbs. (As you rub the butter into the flour, lift it up high and let it fall back into the bowl.) Alternatively, pulse the mixture in a food processor until the mixture resembles fine breadcrumbs.

■ Make a well in the center, add the chilled water and mix with a flat-bladed knife, using a cutting action rather than a stirring action, until the mixture comes together in beads. Add a little extra water if needed to bring the dough together.

■ Gather the dough, press gently together into a ball, and flatten slightly into a disc. Wrap in plastic wrap and refrigerate for 30 minutes before using.

■ Homemade shortcrust pastry can be covered in plastic wrap and stored in the fridge for 2–3 days, or frozen for 2–3 months.

To make a sweet shortcrust pastry, add 1 tablespoon of confectioners' sugar to the flour. Add 1 beaten egg yolk and only 2–3 tablespoons of chilled water to the mixture and then follow the basic recipe.

—

The easiest way to roll out the pastry is to place the ball of dough between two sheets of baking paper and use a large rolling pin. The paper prevents the dough sticking to the surface and makes it easier to handle.

MAKES ENOUGH FOR 1 TWO-CRUST PIE (8")

pea soup.

This is a simple and modern version of an old favorite—pea and ham soup. The ham bone is replaced with bacon and I use fresh or frozen peas instead of the traditional dried variety. This soup is delicious served hot or cold.

1 tablespoon olive oil
2 slices bacon, roughly chopped
1 onion, roughly chopped
1 rib celery, roughly chopped
1 leek, sliced

4 cups chicken stock
(see page 39) or vegetable stock
1 pound fresh or frozen peas
1 tablespoon roughly chopped mint
salt and freshly ground black pepper

■ Heat the oil in a large saucepan over medium heat. Add the bacon and cook, stirring occasionally, for 2 minutes. Add the onion, celery, and leek, and cook, stirring constantly, for 4–5 minutes, or until the vegetables are tender but have not browned. Add the stock and bring to the a boil. Reduce the heat and simmer for 15 minutes. Add the peas, return to a boil, and then simmer for 10 minutes.

■ Remove from the heat and allow to cool a little. Purée the soup in batches in a blender or with a handheld blender until smooth. Season to taste with salt and freshly ground black pepper. Serve garnished with mint.

For a vegetarian version of this soup, omit the bacon and use vegetable stock.

SERVES 4

pecan pie.

1 sweet shortcrust pastry
(see page 119)

1½ cups pecans

7 tablespoons unsalted butter, melted

½ cup honey or golden syrup

½ cup lightly packed brown sugar

3 eggs

½ teaspoon mixed spice

finely grated zest and juice of 1 lemon

- Prepare the pastry according to the instructions on page 119. Chill the pastry for at least 30 minutes before using.

- Lightly grease a 10" loose-based tart pan. Roll out the pastry between two sheets of baking paper so that it is large enough to fit the tart pan. Line the pan with the pastry, leaving a little pastry overhanging the pan. Refrigerate for 15 minutes.

- Preheat the oven to 400°F.

- Line the pastry shell with baking paper. Half-fill the pastry shell with pie weights, uncooked dried beans or rice, and bake for 12 minutes. Remove the weights and baking paper, return the pan to the oven and cook for 10–15 minutes longer, or until the pastry is dry and lightly colored. Set aside to cool. If the pastry shell has any holes, plug them with a little uncooked pastry. With a sharp knife, cut off the overhanging pastry.

- Reduce the oven temperature to 350°F.

- Roughly chop half the pecans and place them in a large mixing bowl. Add the melted butter, honey, sugar, eggs, spice, lemon zest and juice and mix well. Pour the mixture into the pastry shell and top with the remaining whole pecans.

- Bake for 25—30 minutes, or until firm. Remove from the oven and allow to cool for at least 20 minutes before removing from the pan. Serve warm or cold with thick cream or ice cream.

SERVES 8-10

peppers, roasted.

red peppers (bell peppers) | **olive oil**

- Preheat the oven to 375°F.

- Brush the peppers with oil and place in a single layer in a baking pan. Place on the top rack of the oven and roast, turning occasionally, for 25–30 minutes, or until the skin is blackened and bubbling. Remove and transfer to a large heatproof bowl. Cover with plastic wrap and set aside to cool.

- When cool, quarter the peppers, discard the seeds and juice, and peel off the skin.

- Use within 2 days or store by placing the pepper quarters in a screw-top jar and filling with enough olive oil to cover. Refrigerate for up to 2 weeks.

Roasted peppers make a great addition to an antipasto platter. It is also delicious added to salads or a frittata or quiche.

—

Chopped fresh herbs or peeled garlic added to a jar of roasted peppers make delicious variations.

pesto.

Purists make pesto by hand in a mortar and pestle, but use a blender
or food processor for a simple and fast result.

⅓ cup pine nuts	3 cloves garlic, roughly chopped
2 cups basil leaves	1 cup extra-virgin olive oil
⅓ cup freshly grated parmesan	salt and freshly ground black pepper

- Place the pine nuts, basil, parmesan, and garlic in a food processor or blender and process until the mixture is roughly chopped.

- With the motor running, slowly add the olive oil in a thin stream, and process until the mixture is smooth but retains some texture. It will remain a good green color so long as it is not overprocessed. Season to taste with salt and freshly ground black pepper. Store in a screw-top jar, cover with a thin film of oil, and keep in the fridge for up to 2 weeks.

Pesto is delicious mixed with a bowl of pasta or gnocchi. A teaspoon added to a bowl of vegetable soup is the perfect finishing touch.

—

Always use a good-quality extra-virgin olive oil and freshly purchased pine nuts for pesto.

MAKES 2 CUPS

pizza base.

Pizza dough is easy to make; it simply needs a little time to rise.

1¼-ounce package (2¼ teaspoons) active dry yeast	2½ cups bread flour
1 teaspoon sugar	salt
	2 tablespoons olive oil

- Dissolve the yeast and sugar in a small bowl with ¾ cup of warm water. Stir well and set aside for 10 minutes, or until the mixture froths.

- Place the flour and a pinch of salt in a large mixing bowl. Make a well in the center and add the yeast mixture and olive oil. Mix until a firm dough forms.

- Knead on a lightly floured surface for 5–7 minutes, or until smooth and elastic. Place in a clean, lightly oiled bowl, cover with a cloth or plastic wrap and leave in a warm place for 1–1½ hours, or until the dough has doubled in size.

- Preheat the oven to 425°F.

- Punch down the dough with your fist to release the air. Divide into two or three equal portions and roll out or press to a thickness of ¼". Transfer to lightly oiled pizza trays.

- Top with your choice of toppings and bake for 15 minutes. Then slide the pizza off the tray onto the oven shelf and cook for 3–4 minutes longer, to crisp up the base.

A good pizza base should have a little bit of chew, so don't roll out the dough any thinner than ¼".

—

Pizza bases can be made and frozen, uncooked, for 2–3 months.
Don't overload your pizzas with toppings—less is definitely more.

MAKES THREE 9" OR TWO 12" PIZZA BASES

pizza marguerita.

Cornmeal, to sprinkle	3 cups mozzarella cheese, shredded
1 homemade pizza base or pizza dough (see page 125)	3 tablespoons extra-virgin olive oil
	12 small basil leaves
3 cups pizza sauce, jarred or homemade	salt and freshly ground black pepper

- Lightly oil two 12" pizza trays or baking sheets and sprinkle each with a little cornmeal.

- Make the pizza dough as described on page 125. After the first rise, punch down the dough and gently knead for one minute.

- Preheat the oven to 475°F.

- Divide the dough into 2 portions. On a lightly floured surface, roll each portion to a 12" diameter circle.

- Transfer the pizza bases to the prepared pizza trays or baking sheets.

- Spread each base with an even layer of sauce. Top each with cheese and drizzle with extra-virgin olive oil. Season to taste with salt and freshly ground black pepper. Bake for 12–15 minutes, or until the crust is golden and the cheese has melted.

- Remove from the oven, drizzle with a little extra oil, and scatter over the basil leaves.

To make an easy tomato pizza sauce, drain two 13-ounce cans of chopped or crushed Italian tomatoes in a fine sieve for about 10 minutes, discarding the liquid. Place the tomato pulp, 2 cloves crushed garlic, 3 tablespoons olive oil, and ½ teaspoon dried oregano in a medium saucepan and cook over low heat, stirring frequently for 20–30 minutes, or until thick. Season to taste with salt and freshly ground black pepper. Store, in a sealed container, in a refrigerator for up to 5 days or freeze any excess for up to 2 months.

MAKES TWO 12" PIZZAS

poached pears.

| 6 firm, ripe pears | ½ cup sugar |
| 1 lemon, halved | 1 cinnamon stick |

- Carefully peel the pears, leaving the stalks attached if possible. Squeeze the juice of half a lemon over the pears as you peel them to stop them from browning.

- Place the peeled pears in a large saucepan. Add enough water to just cover. Remove the pears and set aside.

- Add the sugar and cinnamon stick to the saucepan. Peel the zest from the remaining lemon half and add the zest to the saucepan. Bring the mixture to a boil, stirring to dissolve the sugar. Return the pears to the saucepan. Bring to a boil again, then reduce the heat and simmer for 15–20 minutes, or until the pears are tender.

- Transfer the pears to a large serving dish. Strain the syrup, discarding the cinnamon and lemon zest, and return to a boil over high heat. Simmer rapidly until it is reduced by half. Pour the syrup over the pears. Serve warm or cold with cream or yogurt.

Poached pears and chocolate are a classic combination.
Serve pears with the chocolate sauce given on page 49.

—

Replacing 1 cup of the poaching water with 1 cup of red wine
makes a delicious variation.

SERVES 6

popcorn.

½ cup popcorn | **2 tablespoons canola oil**

■ Use a large heavy saucepan with a tight-fitting lid. Place over medium heat for 30 seconds.

■ Add the oil, wait 10 seconds, then add the popcorn. Stir to coat the kernels with oil then quickly put the lid on. Give the pan a good shake.

■ The corn will begin to pop. Be sure to keep the lid on and the pan over the heat while cooking. Keep shaking the pot, holding the lid in place until the corn is all popped—it will take about 3–4 minutes.

■ Empty the popcorn into a bowl and serve sprinkled with salt or sugar.

To make spiced popcorn, melt 4 tablespoons of butter in a small saucepan, stir in ½ teaspoon of cayenne pepper and then pour over the hot popcorn, mixing well until combined.

—

To make a sweet version, melt 4 tablespoons of butter in a small saucepan, stir in 2 tablespoons of honey and ½ teaspoon of ground cinnamon, then pour over the hot popcorn, mixing well until combined.

SERVES 4

popovers.

2 cups plain (all-purpose) flour

½ teaspoon salt

3 eggs, lightly beaten

2 cups milk

1 tablespoon vegetable oil or melted butter

oil, to cook

- Combine the flour and salt into a bowl.

- In another bowl, combine the beaten eggs, milk, and oil.

- Gradually pour the wet mixture into the dry mixture, beating with a wooden spoon until smooth.

- Allow the batter to rest for at least 1 hour.

- Preheat the oven to 450°F.

- Using a 12-cup muffin or popover pan, place ½ teaspoon of oil into each individual muffin cup. Place in a hot oven for 5 minutes, or until the oil is very hot and smoking.

- Pour the batter into the muffin cups, leaving ½" space at the top. Bake in the top half of the oven for 15–20 minutes, or until risen and golden. Don't be tempted to open the oven before they're ready, otherwise they will collapse.

Resting the batter is crucial. It allows the starch in the flour to swell, which bursts when it hits the hot oil, giving the popover a light texture.

—

For cheese popovers, add ⅓ cup of grated cheddar cheese to the batter before baking.

SERVES 12

pork, roasted with crackling.

The best crackling comes from the hindquarters, so choose either a pork leg or loin to roast. Ask your butcher to score the skin for you.

1 pork leg or loin (3 pounds)	6 cloves garlic, unpeeled
salt and freshly ground black pepper	2 pounds potatoes, peeled and cut into chunks
3 sprigs rosemary	

- Preheat the oven to 425°F.

- Pat the pork dry with kitchen paper and rub the scored skin well with salt. Season with freshly ground pepper.

- Place the pork, skin-side up, in a roasting pan and tuck the rosemary and garlic underneath. Roast for 20 minutes.

- Reduce the heat to 350°F and continue to roast for 1 hour.

- Add the potatoes to the roasting pan, turning occasionally, for 1 hour longer, or until the potatoes are tender inside and crisp on the outside. To test if the meat is done, insert a sharp knife or metal skewer into the center—the juice should run clear. Remove the pork, cut away the crackling, and return it to the top shelf of the oven if it needs further cooking. Cover the meat and potatoes with foil and set aside to rest for 10 minutes.

- To make gravy, refer to the instructions on page 91.

- To serve, carve the pork into slices and accompany with potatoes, crackling, gravy, and apple sauce.

Calculate the cooking time for different pork cuts by allowing 30 minutes for every 1 pound, plus an extra 30 minutes.

SERVES 4-6

pot of tea.

Throw out your teabags and return to the ritual of a *real* cuppa made from tea leaves! Personal taste, the strength of the brand of tea, and the size of the pot will determine how much tea to use. As a guide, start by adding 2–3 teaspoons of tea leaves for an average-sized two-person pot.

■ Fill a kettle with fresh cold water and bring to a boil. When the water has almost reached a boil, pour a little into your teapot, swirl it around and pour it out. Add 2–3 teaspoons of tea leaves to the pot.

■ When the water is boiling, fill the teapot with boiling water. Put on the lid and leave to brew for 3–5 minutes.

■ The pot may be topped up later with more boiling water if needed.

Experiment by trying different types of tea. Look out for a specialist tea shop. Black tea varieties include Orange Pekoe, Darjeeling, Assam, and blended varieties like English Breakfast and Earl Grey. These teas are dried and fermented to produce a dark-colored leaf.

—

Green tea is made from the same plant as black tea but is not fermented. If making green tea, use water that has not quite come to a boil.

—

Serve full-flavored teas such as Assam or English Breakfast in the morning. Orange Pekoe and Darjeeling are lighter, more aromatic teas and are perfect for an afternoon cuppa.

SERVES 2

potato and leek soup.

2 tablespoons vegetable oil

2 large leeks, washed and white parts sliced into rounds

2 ribs celery, chopped

2 pounds potatoes, peeled and roughly diced

5 cups chicken stock

4 tablespoons cream

4 slices bacon

1 tablespoon chopped fresh chives

- Heat the oil over medium heat in a large saucepan. Add the leeks and celery and cook, stirring occasionally, for 2 minutes. Add the potatoes and cook, stirring, for 4–5 minutes, or until the leeks are soft, but not browned.

- Add the stock and bring to a boil. Reduce the heat and simmer for 30 minutes, or until the vegetables are tender.

- Remove from the heat and leave to cool slightly. Puree the soup in batches in a food processor until smooth. Season to taste with salt and freshly ground black pepper.

- Return to the stove, add the cream and gently reheat (do not bring to a boil).

- Broil the bacon until crisp and then roughly chop.

- Ladle the hot soup into bowls and garnish with the chopped bacon and chives.

For a vegetarian version, use vegetable stock and omit the bacon.

SERVES 4

potato gratin.

2½ cups cream

1 bay leaf

salt and freshly ground black pepper

3 pounds russet potatoes, peeled

2 cloves garlic, finely chopped

- Preheat the oven to 325°F. Grease a large, shallow ovenproof dish.

- Place the cream and bay leaf in a large saucepan and season with freshly ground black pepper. Slowly bring to a boil, then simmer gently for 10 minutes. Remove the bay leaf.

- Slice the potatoes very thinly. Add the slices to the saucepan, stir well, and return the mixture to a boil. Simmer for 2–3 minutes, stirring gently.

- Spoon a third of the potato mixture into the prepared dish, sprinkle with salt, pepper, and a little chopped garlic. Repeat until the dish is full. Cover with foil and bake for 1 hour. Remove the foil and bake for 15–20 minutes longer, or until the top is golden and bubbling and the potato is tender.

SERVES 6

potato, mashed.

2 pounds potatoes, peeled and
cut into chunks
1 cup milk

½ cup butter, cubed
salt and freshly ground black pepper

- Place the potato pieces in a large saucepan of salted water. Bring to a boil and cook for 20–25 minutes, or until tender. Drain and return the potatoes to the saucepan. Cook over low heat for 1–2 minutes to remove any remaining moisture.

- Meanwhile, heat the milk in a small saucepan over medium heat.

- Mash the potatoes with the butter and ¾ cup of the hot milk until smooth. Beat well with a wooden spoon to fluff up the potato, adding a little more milk if needed. The mash should be soft and fluffy. Season to taste with salt and freshly ground black pepper.

The best mashed potato is made from varieties that are high in starch.
Choose varieties such as russet, yukon gold, or red bliss potatoes.

—

If you like a coarse texture to your mash, use a potato masher. Or for a really light,
fluffy mash, push the potatoes through a mouli or potato ricer.

—

Try adding other vegetables, such as parsnip, celeriac, or sweet potato, to the mash.

—

Add some gruyère cheese or pesto for a variation on standard mashed potato.

SERVES 4-6

potatoes, roasted.

A perfect roast potato is crisp on the outside and soft and fluffy on the inside.

2 pounds russet or red bliss potatoes | **salt**
2-3 tablespoons olive oil |

- Preheat the oven to 400°F.

- Peel and cut the potatoes into even-sized pieces. Cook in a large saucepan of boiling salted water for 8–10 minutes, or until just tender. Drain well and return to the saucepan. Shake well in the pan, or use a fork to roughen up the surfaces a bit. (Rough edges help the potatoes to become crisp.)

- Pour the oil into a baking dish and place in the hot oven for 5 minutes. Remove the dish and add the potatoes. Stir to coat with the oil. Season well with salt.

- Roast on the top shelf of the oven, turning occasionally, for 50–60 minutes, or until crisp and golden. Serve with your favorite roast meat.

Potatoes absorb less fat and cook faster if placed in a hot baking dish with hot oil.

—

As a variation, add 3–4 unpeeled garlic cloves and 1 tablespoon of chopped rosemary 10 minutes before the end of the cooking time. Or try chopped bacon stirred into the potatoes 7–10 minutes before the end of the cooking time.

SERVES 4-6

potato salad.

2 pounds waxy potatoes, scrubbed

2-3 tablespoons chopped flat-leaf
parsley, chives, or mint

4 finely sliced scallions

½ small red onion, finely sliced

salt and freshly ground black pepper

6 slices prosciutto or bacon

DRESSING

½ cup olive oil

1 tablespoon Dijon mustard

2 tablespoons white wine vinegar

- Cook the potatoes in a large saucepan of gently boiling salted water for 12–15 minutes, or until just tender. Drain and allow to cool slightly.

- While the potatoes are still warm, cut them into ¾" pieces and place in a large bowl with the parsley, scallions, and red onion. Season well with salt and freshly ground black pepper.

- Place the dressing ingredients in a screw-top jar and shake well to combine. Pour half the dressing over the warm potatoes and toss gently to coat the pieces, being careful not to break up the potato. Allow to stand until most of the dressing is absorbed.

- Meanwhile, cook the prosciutto or bacon in a frying pan or under a broiler until crisp. Prosciutto should take 3–4 minutes, bacon 5–7 minutes. Allow to cool, then break into bite-sized pieces.

- Gently stir half the prosciutto or bacon into the salad. Transfer to a serving dish, drizzle with the remaining dressing, and sprinkle over the remaining prosciutto or bacon. Serve warm or at room temperature.

For best results, use medium-sized, waxy potatoes such as round white and round red or small new potatoes when available.

SERVES 4-6

pumpkin soup.

2 tablespoons vegetable oil

1 large onion, chopped

1 carrot, chopped

1 clove garlic, chopped

2 potatoes, peeled and chopped

1 pound peeled and chopped pumpkin

5 cups chicken stock (see page 39)

salt and freshly ground black pepper

yogurt or sour cream, to serve

- Heat the oil in a large saucepan over medium heat. Add the onion, carrot, garlic, potato, and pumpkin. Cook, stirring, for 5 minutes, or until the onion has softened.

- Add the stock and bring to a boil. Cover and simmer for 25–30 minutes, or until the vegetables are tender.

- Allow to cool a little, then purée the mixture in batches in a blender or with a handheld blender.

- Gently reheat the soup. Season to taste with salt and freshly ground black pepper. Serve garnished with a dollop of yogurt.

For an Asian-inspired soup, cook the vegetables with 1 tablespoon of Thai red curry paste. Stir in ½ cup of coconut milk before serving.

SERVES 4

raspberry sauce.

1¼ cups fresh raspberries

¼ cup confectioners' sugar, sifted

1 tablespoon lemon juice

1–2 tablespoons raspberry-flavored brandy or raspberry-flavored liqueur (optional)

- Purée the raspberries, confectioners' sugar, and lemon juice in a blender or food processor. Stir in the alcohol, if using. Pass the sauce through a strainer to remove any seeds.

- Taste and add extra lemon juice or sugar if needed.

- This sauce is good served with ice cream, fresh or cooked fruit, chocolate cake, bavarian cream, pannacotta, or tarts.

Thawed, frozen berries work equally well.

—

Replace the raspberries with an equal quantity of strawberries, blackberries, or blueberries for a different berry sauce.

—

To make a mango sauce, use the flesh of two large ripe mangoes and follow the recipe above.

MAKES 1½ CUPS

ratatouille.

Although not traditional, this is my favorite way to make ratatouille.

2 tablespoons olive oil	1 13-ounce can chopped tomatoes
1 onion, chopped	salt and freshly ground black pepper
2 cloves garlic, chopped	2 tablespoons roughly chopped basil
2 zucchini, sliced	1 tablespoon lemon juice
1 eggplant, diced	extra-virgin olive oil, to serve
1 large bell pepper, seeded and chopped	

■ Heat the olive oil in a large frying pan and fry the onion and garlic over medium heat for 10 minutes, or until soft. Add the zucchini, eggplant, and pepper and cook for 10 minutes longer, stirring occasionally. Stir in the tomatoes, cover and simmer, stirring occasionally, for 10 minutes.

■ Season with salt and freshly ground black pepper. Stir in the basil and lemon juice and remove from the heat.

■ Serve ratatouille hot or cold, drizzled with a little extra-virgin olive oil.

Ratatouille is delicious served with roast meat, or as a filling for vegetarian lasagna. It also makes a great pasta sauce.

SERVES 4

rhubarb and apple crumble.

1 bunch rhubarb	¾ cup lightly packed brown sugar
4 granny smith apples, peeled, cored and chopped	½ teaspoon ground ginger
¾ cup sugar	½ cup unsalted butter, chilled and diced
juice of 1 lemon	¼ cup sliced almonds
1 cup plain (all-purpose) flour	

- Grease a 4-cup-capacity ovenproof dish.

- Trim the rhubarb and cut the stems into 1" lengths; enough for 3-4 cups. Set aside.

- Heat a frying pan or large saucepan over medium heat and add the apples, sugar, and lemon juice. Cook, stirring, for 3–4 minutes, or until tender.

- Add the chopped rhubarb and cook for 4–5 minutes, or until the rhubarb is tender but still holds its shape. The rhubarb will give off a lot of liquid.

- Use a slotted spoon to transfer the cooked fruit to the prepared dish. Leave behind any liquid remaining in the frying pan. Allow the fruit to cool a little. Taste and add extra sugar if needed.

- Preheat the oven to 350°F.

- With your fingertips, rub together the flour, brown sugar, ginger, and butter until the mixture resembles breadcrumbs and starts to clump together. Mix in the sliced almonds.

- Sprinkle the crumble mixture evenly over the fruit. Bake for 30 minutes, or until golden and bubbling. Serve with cream or ice cream.

Rhubarb is generally at its peak from April to June. When choosing rhubarb, look for crisp red stalks; the deeper the color, the sweeter the flavor.

—

Be careful to trim away any leaves from the rhubarb, as they are poisonous. If rhubarb is unavailable, try using strawberries as a variation.

SERVES 4 - 6

rice.

To make the perfect fluffy rice, use the absorption method. Choose long-grain rice such as basmati that will separate into fluffy individual grains when cooked. This makes a delicious accompaniment to braised food, Indian dishes, or roast meats.

1 cup long-grain rice | **salt**

■ Place 2¼ cups of water, the rice, and ½ teaspoon of salt in a large saucepan and bring to a boil over high heat. Stir once, then reduce the heat to the lowest setting and cover with a tight-fitting lid. Cook for 15 minutes. Check that all the water has been absorbed. If not, cook for a couple of minutes longer. Remove from the heat and allow to rest, covered, for 5–10 minutes. Fluff the rice with a fork before serving.

Use ¼ cup of rice and ½ cup of water per person.

—

Don't be tempted to stir the rice while it cooks, as this releases the starch in the grain and makes it sticky.

—

Serve rice plain or tossed with herbs, spices, or cooked vegetables.

SERVES 4

rice, fried.

The recipe for this favorite Cantonese dish can be readily varied, depending on what ingredients are at hand.

1 tablespoon vegetable oil	1 tablespoon grated fresh ginger
2 eggs, lightly beaten	1 cup shredded Chinese barbecue pork
2 tablespoons peanut oil	4 cups cooked rice, chilled
5 scallions, chopped	1 tablespoon soy sauce
1 clove garlic, crushed	salt and ground white pepper
½ cup frozen peas, thawed	

- Heat the vegetable oil in a moderately hot wok and add the beaten egg, swirling it around to coat the wok. When set, turn out onto a board and allow to cool. Cut into strips.

- Heat the peanut oil in the wok. Add the scallions, garlic, peas, and ginger. Stir-fry for 2–3 minutes. Add the pork and allow to warm through. Add the rice and egg strips. Stir-fry vigorously, breaking up any lumps of rice, until heated through. Add the soy sauce and mix until well combined. Season with salt and ground white pepper and serve immediately.

Always begin with cold rice cooked the day before. Boil 2 cups of long-grain rice in a large saucepan of boiling salted water for 10–15 minutes, or until tender. When cooked, drain and rinse. Store overnight in the refrigerator.

—

Chinese barbecue pork is available in Asian food stores and restaurants. If it is unavailable, substitute chopped cooked ham, chopped cooked bacon, or chopped cooked chicken.

—

Peeled, cooked shrimp added toward the end of the cooking time is also delicious in this dish.

SERVES 4

rice pudding.

3 cups milk	½ cup short-grain rice, pudding rice, or arborio rice
1 cup cream	
finely grated zest of 1 orange	⅓ cup sugar
3 cardamom pods	

- Combine the milk, cream, and orange zest in a medium-sized saucepan.

- Remove the seeds from the cardamom pods and crush them with the back of a knife. Add the crushed seeds to the saucepan.

- Bring the mixture to a boil over medium heat. Reduce the heat to low, add the rice and sugar, and stir well until the sugar has dissolved. Simmer, stirring frequently to prevent the rice from sticking, for 30–35 minutes, or until the rice is soft and creamy and the mixture has thickened. Remove from the heat, cover, and set aside for 15 minutes. Spoon into a large serving dish or into individual decorative dishes. Serve warm or cold.

Short-grain rice is traditionally used for rice pudding because the starch breaks down easily as it is cooked, giving the pudding a delicious creamy texture.

—

It is important to stir the rice frequently as it cooks. This helps to release the starch in the grains as well as to prevent the rice sticking to the pan.

—

Rice pudding is delicious served as it is or accompanied with fresh berries, orange segments, or poached stone fruit.

SERVES 4-6

risotto.

5 cups chicken stock (see page 39) or vegetable stock

3 tablespoons butter

1 onion, finely chopped

1½ cups arborio rice

⅓ cup dry white wine

½ cup freshly grated parmesan

- Bring the stock to a gentle simmer in a large saucepan.

- Meanwhile, heat 2 tablespoons of the butter in a large, heavy-based saucepan. Add the onion and cook, stirring, over moderate heat for 5 minutes, or until soft. The onion should soften but not change color. Add the rice to the onion and stir gently for 2 minutes to coat the grains with a little butter. Add the wine. Stir and allow most of the liquid to evaporate.

- Add the simmering stock, a ladleful at a time, to the rice mixture. The first amount of stock added should just cover the rice. Allow the rice to absorb the liquid before more stock is added. Stir frequently, and add more stock as required. It will take 18–25 minutes to cook. Taste the rice for texture—it should be soft but still retain a little bite.

- Remove from the heat and add the remaining 1 tablespoon of butter and the grated parmesan. Cover and allow to rest for 5 minutes before serving.

The grains should fall easily from a spoon, and the liquid thicken to a creamy consistency. If necessary, moisten the risotto with a little more stock just before serving.

—

You can add almost anything you like to risotto. Try different combinations of herbs, sautéed mushrooms, cooked vegetables, cooked meats, and seafood. Add ingredients toward the end of cooking.

—

Don't be tempted to leave out the butter at the end. Called "mantecare," this process of adding the butter softens and marries all the flavors.

—

The better the stock, the better the risotto. Try homemade stock, such as chicken stock (see page 39).

SERVES 4

salmon, poached with salsa verde.

4 salmon fillets

salt and freshly ground black pepper

SALSA VERDE

1 thick slice Italian-style bread

milk, to soak

1 cup loosely packed flat-leaf parsley

15 basil leaves

1 tablespoon capers

2 anchovy fillets

1 clove garlic, chopped

¼ cup olive oil

- To make the salsa verde, remove the crust from the bread, break the bread into pieces and soak it in a little milk. Squeeze dry and set aside.

- In a food processor or blender, process the parsley, basil, capers, anchovies, and garlic until roughly chopped. Add the milk-soaked bread. With the machine running, gradually add the olive oil in a thin stream, and process until the sauce is thick and smooth. Season to taste with salt and freshly ground black pepper.

- Lay a salmon fillet, skin-side down, on a sheet of foil. Season well with salt and freshly ground black pepper. Wrap the fillet tightly in the foil, making an airtight seal. Repeat with the remaining fillets.

- Place the wrapped fillets in a large saucepan and cover completely with cold water. Bring to a boil over medium heat. Reduce the heat and simmer gently for 2 minutes.

- Remove the parcels from the saucepan. Open each one and remove the skin from the fish. Serve the salmon with the salsa verde, plus steamed potatoes and a mixed green salad.

SERVES 4

salt and pepper squid.

1¼ pounds cleaned and prepared squid or calamari tubes

½ cup plain (all-purpose) flour or rice flour

2 tablespoons sea salt

1 tablespoon freshly ground black pepper

1 teaspoon chili powder

1 medium-sized red chili, finely chopped

vegetable oil, to fry

- Rinse the squid. Cut along each side of the body so it opens out flat. Dry well with kitchen paper. Score the skin with a sharp knife and cut into either ½" wide strips or 2" diamonds.

- In a shallow dish, combine the flour, sea salt, pepper, chili powder, and chopped chili. Dip the pieces of squid into the flour mixture and toss to coat. Shake off any excess.

- Pour vegetable oil into a large frying pan or wok to a depth of ¾". Heat the oil to 350°F—a cube of bread dropped in the oil should brown in 15 seconds.

- Cook the squid in batches in the hot oil for 1–2 minutes, or until golden. Remove with tongs or a slotted spoon and drain on crumpled kitchen paper. Taste and season with a little extra salt and pepper if necessary. This dish should taste salty and spicy.

- Serve with lemon or lime wedges.

Replace half the ground black pepper with 2 teaspoons of ground Sichuan peppercorns for an interesting flavor variation.

—

A pinch of Chinese five-spice powder is good added to the salt and pepper mix. Peeled uncooked shrimp is also good prepared this way.

SERVES 4

150

seafood chowder.

2 tablespoons olive oil

1 onion, sliced

4 medium-sized potatoes, peeled and diced

2 tablespoons plain (all-purpose) flour

5 cups fish stock or vegetable stock

½ cup dry white wine

1 bay leaf

3 sprigs thyme

1 pound firm white fish fillets

½ pound smoked fish (haddock or cod) fillets

1 pound medium-sized uncooked shrimp, peeled and deveined

1 cup cream or milk

salt and freshly ground black pepper

2 tablespoons chopped flat-leaf parsley or chervil

- Heat the oil in a large saucepan, add the onion and potatoes and cook gently, without browning, until the onion is soft and translucent. Sprinkle over the flour and cook, stirring, for 1 minute.

- Add the stock, wine, bay leaf, and thyme and stir until smooth. Bring to a boil, reduce the heat, and simmer for 10–15 minutes, or until the potatoes are soft. Remove the bay leaf and thyme.

- Skin the white fish fillets and cut into bite-sized chunks. Break the smoked fish into bite-sized pieces. Add the fish and shrimp to the saucepan and simmer for 3–4 minutes, or until the fish is opaque and the shrimp have turned pink.

- Stir in the cream or milk and heat slowly without bringing to a boil. Season well with salt and freshly ground black pepper. Sprinkle over the parsley or chervil and serve.

SERVES 6

shortbread.

1 cup unsalted butter, softened	2 cups plain (all-purpose) flour
½ cup sugar	½ cup rice flour

- Preheat the oven to 300°F. Line two oven trays with baking paper.

- Beat the butter in a bowl with a wooden spoon until soft and smooth. Add the sugar, plain flour, and rice flour and work the mixture with the spoon until blended.

- Knead the dough lightly on a floured surface to form a firm dough, then chill for 20 minutes.

- Divide the dough into two portions and roll out each between two sheets of baking paper to a thickness of ¼–⅓". Cut the dough into shapes with cookie cutters. Place the shapes onto the prepared oven trays and bake for 15–20 minutes, or until pale and dry. Alternatively, roll out each portion of dough to form a circle 7" in diameter. Mark each circle into wedges with a knife, prick the surface several times with a fork, sprinkle with a little extra sugar, and bake for 35–40 minutes, or until pale and dry. Store shortbread in an airtight container for up to 1 week.

Shortbread should be dry with a melt-in-the-mouth texture.

—

Rice flour gives the shortbread a wonderful grainy texture.

—

As a variation, add a little grated or finely chopped citrus zest to the dough.

MAKES 35-40 COOKIES OR 2 LARGE ROUNDS

spaghetti with garlic, chili, and oil.

This is the simplest and speediest of all pasta dishes. Olive oil is infused with garlic and chili, which is then stirred into hot pasta. This dish fills the kitchen with the heady aroma of garlic.

1 pound dried spaghetti	1–2 large red chilies, seeded and finely chopped
⅓ cup olive oil	2 tablespoons chopped flat-leaf parsley
4 cloves garlic, finely chopped	salt and freshly ground black pepper

- Bring a large saucepan of salted water to a boil and add the spaghetti. Stir well and boil rapidly for 8 minutes, or until the spaghetti is al dente.

- Meanwhile, combine the oil, garlic, and chili in a small saucepan. Cook over very low heat for 7–8 minutes to allow the oil to absorb the chili and garlic flavors. The oil should barely simmer. The garlic should color slightly, but don't allow it to burn.

- Drain the cooked pasta and return it to the large saucepan over moderate heat. Pour over the oil mixture and add the parsley. Toss thoroughly with two forks to coat the pasta with the oil. Season with salt and freshly ground black pepper. Serve immediately.

Allow 4 ounces of dried spaghetti per person.

—

You can vary this dish by using chopped basil or arugula in place of the parsley. A squeeze of lemon juice is also delicious.

—

If you like, serve with freshly grated parmesan.

SERVES 4

spiced nuts.

3 cups unsalted mixed nuts	¼ teaspoon cayenne pepper
2 tablespoons olive oil	½ teaspoon ground turmeric
1 tablespoon brown sugar	freshly ground black pepper (optional)
2 tablespoons sea salt	

- Combine all of the ingredients in a mixing bowl. Add a little extra cayenne pepper and a grinding of black pepper if you prefer a spicier mix.

- Place in a large frying pan and toast, stirring frequently, over moderate heat for 5–7 minutes, or until golden. Taste and season with a little extra salt if desired.

- Allow to cool and serve in small bowls as a snack. Spiced nuts make a perfect accompaniment to a drink or two. Once completely cool, store the nuts in an airtight container for up to 1 week.

Make a mixture of your personal favorites. Try macadamias, pecans, cashews, and Brazil nuts.

—

A tablespoon of toasted sesame seeds stirred through the mix makes a delicious addition.

MAKES 2 CUPS

sponge cake.

1½ cups plain (all-purpose) flour, sifted
¾ teaspoon baking powder
⅛ teaspoon salt
5 tablespoons unsalted butter, melted
6 eggs
¼ cup sugar

1 teaspoon vanilla extract
1 cup berry jam
1 cup cream
½ teaspoon vanilla extract
confectioners' sugar, to dust

- Preheat oven to 350°F. Grease two 8" shallow round cake pans and line the base of each with baking paper.

- In a small bowl, combine the sifted flour, baking powder, and salt.

- In a small saucepan, melt the butter and allow to cool. Set aside.

- Combine the eggs, sugar, and vanilla in a large heatproof bowl. Place the bowl over a saucepan of gently simmering water, making sure the base of the bowl doesn't touch the water. Beat with an electric mixer on high-speed for 6–7 minutes, or until pale, thick, and doubled in bulk. Remove from the heat and continue to beat for 3 minutes.

- Using a large metal spoon, gently fold in the sifted flour mixture, followed by the cooled melted butter. Mix until just combined and there is no trace of white flour.

- It is important to fold in the flour and butter very gently. If you are too vigorous at this stage, you will lose a lot of volume in the egg mixture.

- Spread the mixture evenly into the prepared pans and bake for 25–30 minutes, or until golden and firm to the touch. Leave to cool in the pans for 5 minutes, then turn out onto a wire rack to cool completely.

- Spread the jam evenly over one of the cakes. Whip the cream and vanilla until soft peaks form, then spoon or pipe the cream over the jam. Top with the remaining cake. Dust with confectioners' sugar.

SERVES 8

steak.

Choose a good cut of aged meat—either a New York cut, sirloin, T-bone, rump or fillet—about 1–1½" thick. Allow about 6½–8 ounces per person. Have the butcher trim off the outer layer of fat.

1 6½–8 ounce steak	freshly ground black pepper
olive oil, to brush	

- Brush one side of the steak with oil and give it a good grinding of black pepper.

- Preheat a heavy-based cast-iron frying pan, grill plate, or barbecue to high heat.

- Sear the steak, oil-side down first, cooking for the desired time (see below). Brush with more oil, give it a good grinding of black pepper, turn the steak over, and cook the other side.

- Remove from the heat, wrap in foil and allow to rest for 5–10 minutes before serving. Serve with herb butter or mustard and a crisp green salad.

For a rare steak, cook 2–3 minutes each side. For medium, cook 3–4 minutes each side. For well done, cook 3 minutes each side, then turn down the heat and cook for 8–10 minutes, turning once.

—

To make herb butter, beat 1 chopped clove of garlic and 2 tablespoons of chopped fresh herbs with ½ cup of softened butter until combined. Roll into a log shape, cover with plastic wrap, and refrigerate until firm. Cut into slices and serve on top of a hot steak.

SERVES 1

sweet chili sauce.

This versatile sauce goes well with chicken, seafood, and meat. Although the recipe contains chilies, sugar is used to take the edge off the heat and give the sauce a pleasant and balanced taste.

¾ cup sugar	6 large red chilies, seeded and roughly chopped
½ cup white vinegar	
1 teaspoon salt	1 tablespoon grated fresh ginger
4 cloves garlic, crushed	1 teaspoon Thai fish sauce

- Place the sugar, vinegar, salt, and 1 cup of water in a small stainless-steel saucepan. Bring to a boil, stirring to dissolve the sugar, and simmer for 5 minutes.

- Add the garlic, chilies, and ginger to the saucepan. Simmer over medium heat, stirring frequently, for 15–20 minutes, or until reduced and thickened. Remove from the heat and add the fish sauce.

- Pulse the mixture in a food processor or blender to produce a sauce with speckles of red chili. Transfer to a clean, sterilized jar and seal. Serve at room temperature. The sauce can be stored in the refrigerator for up to 1 month.

Using large red chilies, which are milder than small ones, allows you to incorporate enough chili to achieve a good red-colored sauce. Add a small red chili if you prefer the sauce a little hotter.

MAKES 1 CUP

thai beef salad.

Thai salads are a combination of opposing tastes and textures—crisp salad leaves, soft noodles and a sweet–sour sauce. Use these principles to create your own combinations.

1 pound beef fillet or rump	DRESSING
3 ounces cellophane noodles	2 tablespoons Thai fish sauce
1 small cucumber, peeled and diced	2 tablespoons lime juice
4 cups mixed salad leaves	1 tablespoon soy sauce
	1 teaspoon vegetable oil
	2 small red chilies, seeded and finely chopped
	2 teaspoons soft brown sugar

- Cook the beef in a hot frying pan or grill pan for 2–3 minutes each side, or until cooked to your liking. Allow to cool.

- Place the cellophane noodles in a heatproof bowl and cover with boiling water. Leave for 6–7 minutes, or until soft. Drain well and cut into $1\frac{1}{4}$" lengths.

- Place the dressing ingredients in a screw-top jar and shake well to combine.

- Slice the beef thinly.

- To serve, mix together the cucumber and salad leaves and place on a large platter or in a large bowl. Top with the noodles and slices of beef. Pour over the dressing.

If time permits, brush the beef with a pounded mixture of 2 garlic cloves, 3 coriander roots, a squeeze of lime juice, and 2 tablespoons of vegetable oil. Marinate for 20 minutes before cooking. The beef may be substituted with lamb fillets, chicken fillets, or baby squid.

SERVES 4

tomato relish.

This relish is deliciously spicy and easy to make. I love it served alongside sausages, cold meats, or cheese. A dollop on a cheese sandwich is perfect.

2 pounds ripe tomatoes	⅓ cup olive oil
1 large onion, finely chopped	1 teaspoon ground ginger
2 cloves garlic, crushed	1 teaspoon ground cumin
2 small red chilies, sliced	1 teaspoon curry powder
1 cup lightly packed brown sugar	salt and freshly ground black pepper
1 cup red wine vinegar	

- Preheat the oven to 275°F.

- Place clean jam jars in the oven to warm.

- Meanwhile, halve the tomatoes and remove the seeds. Roughly chop the tomatoes and place in a saucepan with the remaining ingredients except the salt and pepper. Bring to a boil, reduce the heat and simmer gently, stirring occasionally, for 50–60 minutes, or until the relish is thick, pulpy, and jamlike. Season well with salt and freshly ground black pepper.

- Pour the relish into warm jam jars and allow to cool. Seal when cold. Store in the fridge for 1 month.

MAKES 3 CUPS

tomato sauce for pasta (pomodoro).

2 tablespoons olive oil	1 tablespoon sugar
2 onions, chopped	2 tablespoons tomato paste
3 cloves garlic, chopped	2 tablespoons finely chopped basil
2 13-ounce cans chopped tomatoes	

- Heat the oil in a large saucepan over medium heat and sauté the onions and garlic for 5 minutes. Add the tomatoes and sugar and bring to a boil. Reduce the heat and simmer gently, stirring occasionally, for 20 minutes, or until soft and pulpy.

- Stir in the tomato paste and basil. Serve as is, or as a purée if you prefer a smoother consistency.

Instead of canned tomatoes you can use 2 pounds of peeled, ripe tomatoes.

SERVES 4

tomato soup.

Tomato soup is an all-time favorite—worthy of serving as a simple Sunday-night meal for family, or as a starter at a fine dinner party for friends.

2 tablespoons olive oil	1 13-ounce can chopped tomatoes
1 onion, chopped	4 cups chicken stock (see page 39) or vegetable stock
1 carrot, chopped	
1 rib celery, chopped	salt and freshly ground black pepper
2 cloves garlic, chopped	1 tablespoon chopped basil, to garnish
1½ pounds ripe tomatoes, quartered	extra-virgin olive oil, to garnish

- Heat the oil in a large saucepan. Sauté the onion, carrot, celery, and garlic for 5 minutes, then add the fresh tomatoes and cook for 3–4 minutes.

- Add the canned tomatoes, stock, and 1 cup of water. Bring to a boil, reduce the heat, and simmer for 30 minutes.

- Remove from the heat and allow to cool a little. Purée the soup in batches in a blender or with a handheld blender.

- Season to taste with salt and freshly ground black pepper.

- Serve hot, garnished with chopped basil and a drizzle of extra-virgin olive oil.

Use the best ripe red tomatoes you can find. If the tomatoes lack flavor, add 1 tablespoon of tomato paste.

—

For a richer version, serve drizzled with a little cream or a dollop of sour cream.

SERVES 4

tomatoes, slow-roasted.

| 8 plum tomatoes | 2 teaspoons thyme leaves |
| olive oil | salt and freshly ground black pepper |

- Preheat the oven to 275°F and lightly grease an oven tray.

- Cut the tomatoes in half lengthwise and place, cut-side up, on the prepared oven tray. Drizzle each tomato half lightly with olive oil, then sprinkle evenly with thyme, salt, and freshly grated black pepper.

- Roast for 1½–2 hours, or until the tomatoes are lightly dried and darkened, but still retain some moisture. Use in salads, as part of sandwich fillings, or tossed through cooked pasta. To store, cover completely with olive oil in a screw-top jar and keep in the refrigerator up to 2 weeks.

Plum tomatoes are flavorful egg-shaped tomatoes that come in red and yellow varieties.

MAKES 16

upside-down pear cake.

4 large ripe pears, peeled, cored, and quartered

⅓ cup unsalted butter, melted

½ cup raw sugar

½ cup unsalted butter, softened at room temperature

1½ cups plain (all-purpose) flour

1 teaspoon baking powder

1 teaspoon ground ginger

1 teaspoon mixed spice

pinch of salt

1 cup brown sugar, firmly packed

⅓ cup buttermilk or milk

2 eggs, beaten

- Preheat the oven to 350°F. Lightly grease the sides of a 9" springform cake pan.

- Pour the melted butter into the pan. Sprinkle the sugar over the butter. Arrange the pears cut-side up in the base of the pan.

- Sift the flour, baking powder, ginger, mixed spice, and salt into a mixing bowl. Add the softened butter and brown sugar. Add the milk and eggs and beat with a wooden spoon or hand-held electric beater until smooth.

- Spoon the batter over the pears in the cake pan.

- Bake for about 60 minutes, or until a wooden skewer inserted into the center of the cake comes out clean. Leave to cool for 15 minutes before placing on a wire rack. Serve warm, accompanied with cream or a side dish of ice cream.

For a variation, try using your favorite seasonal fruit such as plum halves, peeled and chopped apples or sliced pineapple rings in place of the pears.

SERVES 8-10

vanilla bean ice cream.

2 cups milk	½ cup sugar
1 vanilla bean	1 cup cream, lightly whipped
6 egg yolks	

- Pour the milk into a small saucepan.

- Using a sharp knife, split the vanilla bean in half lengthwise. Scrape out the seeds and add the pod and the seeds to the saucepan of milk. Bring the mixture to a simmer over low heat.

- In a large mixing bowl, whisk together the egg yolks and sugar for 4–5 minutes, or until the sugar has dissolved and the mixture is thick and pale. Gently whisk the hot milk mixture, including the vanilla bean pod, into the yolk mixture.

- Return this mixture to the saucepan and cook over low heat, stirring constantly with a wooden spoon, until the mixture thickens slightly and coats the back of the spoon. Do not allow the mixture to boil or it will curdle. Remove from the heat and strain into a bowl, discarding the bean pod. Set aside to cool.

- When cold, whisk in the whipped cream. Churn in an ice-cream machine until firm.

- Before serving, soften the ice cream by placing in the fridge for 15 minutes.

SERVES 4-6

vietnamese dipping sauce.

Few tables in southeast Asia are without a little dish of this Vietnamese chili dipping sauce known as *nuoc cham*. It is used as a dip for spring rolls and crudités, and to add flavor and heat to noodle and rice dishes. The flavor should be a balance of sweet, sour, salt, chili, and garlic.

¼ cup fish sauce
1 tablespoon white vinegar
2 tablespoons lime juice
2 teaspoons soft brown sugar

2 large red chilies, seeded and thinly sliced
2 cloves garlic, finely chopped
½ small carrot, coarsely grated (optional)

■ Combine the fish sauce, vinegar, lime juice, and 1 tablespoon of water in a small bowl. Add the sugar and stir to dissolve. Add the chilies and garlic. A coarsely grated carrot is often added to give the sauce crunch. Stir well and serve immediately.

As a variation, try adding 1–2 teaspoons of chopped fresh cilantro leaves or 1 sliced scallion.

—

Remember, there are no fixed rules with this sauce. Taste as you go and adjust the balance of flavors to suit you.

—

Nuoc cham is best made just prior to serving. If made ahead, the chili flavor can often dominate.

MAKES ¾ CUP

yogurt, frozen strawberry.

Easy to make, ultra refreshing, and full of flavor, this yogurt-based ice cream can also be made with low-fat yogurt and without using an ice cream machine.

2 cups strawberries, hulled and roughly chopped ½ cup confectioners' sugar, sifted	juice of 1 lime ½ cup plain yogurt

■ Place the strawberries, lime juice, confectioners' sugar, and yogurt into a blender and puree until smooth. Taste and add extra lemon juice or sugar if desired. Freeze in an ice-cream machine following manufacturer's instructions. If you don't have a machine, pour into a shallow lidded container, place in the freezer for about 2 hours, or until firm and frozen around the edges. Transfer to a food processor and puree until smooth. Return to the freezer until set. Puree the mixture again and return to the freezer one more time. Keep frozen and covered until ready to use for up to 2 weeks. Soften the frozen yogurt by transferring to the refrigerator about 20 minutes before serving. When ready to use, scoop the yogurt into a bowl and serve with fresh fruit or place the yogurt into a cone.

For a light, tropical version—replace the strawberries with 2½ cups of fresh cubed mango or for a decadent treat, try a "raspberry ripple"—Combine 2 cups of plain yogurt with 1 cup of confectioners' sugar, 2 teaspoons of vanilla extract and ½ cup of cream. Mix and freeze until just frozen. Make a puree by combining ½ cup of fresh raspberries with 3 tablespoons of confectioners' sugar and swirl through the frozen yogurt. For a finishing touch, try some shaved chocolate on top.

SERVES 4

conversions.

All cup and spoon measurements are level.

I use large eggs.

All recipes were tested using a conventional oven. If you are using a convection (or fan-forced) oven, set your oven temperature to approximately 70°F lower than is recommended in the recipe.

CUP CONVERSIONS

1 cup uncooked arborio rice = 220 g (7 oz)

1 cup uncooked basmati/long-grain rice = 200 g (6$\frac{1}{2}$ oz)

1 cup sugar = 250 g (8 oz)

1 cup brown sugar = 185 g (6 oz)

1 cup confectioners' sugar = 250 g (8 oz)

1 cup chopped pecans = 125 g (4 oz)

1 cup plain or self-raising (self-rising) flour = 150 g (5 oz)

1 cup cornstarch = 150 g (5 oz)

1 cup uncooked couscous = 180 g (6 oz)

1 cup shredded mozzarella = 150 g (5 oz)

1 cup grated parmesan = 100 g (3$\frac{1}{2}$ oz)

LIQUID CONVERSIONS-

metric	imperial	standard cups
30 ml	1 fl oz	2 tablespoons
60 ml	2 fl oz	$\frac{1}{4}$ cup
80 ml	2$\frac{3}{4}$ fl oz	$\frac{1}{3}$ cup
125 ml	4 fl oz	$\frac{1}{2}$ cup
185 ml	6 fl oz	$\frac{3}{4}$ cup
250 ml	8 fl oz	1 cup

DRY MEASUREMENTS

METRIC	IMPERIAL
15 g	$\frac{1}{2}$ oz
30 g	1 oz
45 g	1$\frac{1}{2}$ oz
55 g	2 oz
125 g	4 oz
150 g	5 oz
200 g	6$\frac{1}{2}$ oz
225 g	7 oz
250 g	8 oz
500 g	1 lb
1 kg	2 lb

OVEN TEMPERATURES

CELSIUS		FAHRENHEIT	GAS MARK
120°C	very slow	250°F	1
150°C	slow	300°F	2
160°C	warm	315°F	2–3
180°C	moderate	350°F	4
190°C	moderately hot	375°F	5
200°C	moderately hot	400°F	6
220°C	hot	425°F	7
230°C	very hot	450°F	8
240°C	very hot	475°F	9

index.